Gay Men of Alcoholics Anonymous:

First-hand Accounts

Also by Robert J. Kus

Keys to Caring: Assisting Your Gay & Lesbian Clients
(Alyson Publications,Inc., 1990)

Gay Men of Alcoholics Anonymous:

First-hand Accounts

Edited by

Robert J. Kus, R.N., Ph.D.

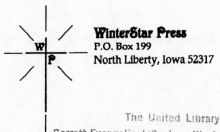

WinterStar Press
P.O. Box 199
North Liberty, Iowa 52317

Printed in The United States of America

First Edition, 1990

Library of Congress Number: 89-052174

ISBN: 0-9625330-0-9

Dedication

To

Douglas J. King

of Chicago

Acknowledgements

Many persons, both known and unknown to me, have worked to make this book possible. I especially wish to thank those persons who put up authors-wanted flyers at gay A.A. round-ups and at A.A. meeting places around the country; Douglas W. Walhovd and Sriram Rao for their secretarial help; Jeff Gimun for formatting and proof-reading; Steven E. Pokorny for serving as assistant editor for the book; A. Lee Rogers and Ken Murdoch for their help in proofreading; Meredith Karns of Morgan-Meredith, Inc. for his help with the cover and formatting; and Francis Fang for his help in formatting the final copy of the book. Most of all, I thank the gay men of Alcoholics Anonymous who took time to write their stories in the hope that their stories would be inspirational to other alcoholics, especially those who are gay men.

Contents

Introduction

In current American thought, alcoholism is viewed as a progressive and incurable disease. It afflicts men more frequently than women, and gay men more frequently than heterosexual men. In fact, some researchers believe that between one-fifth to one-third of gay American men are afflicted with alcoholism. Given the idea that 10% of the United States population has a same-sex sexual orientation - 14% of the men and 6% of the women - the number of gay alcoholic men numbers in the millions. That is the bad news.

There is good news too. Although alcoholism is seen as incurable, it can be arrested. And for hundreds of thousands of gay American men, living the program of Alcoholics Anonymous has been the easiest way to not only achieve abstinence from alcohol and other mind-altering drugs, but to achieve and maintain sobriety, a state of being in which mind, body, and especially spirit grow and flourish.

Conservative estimates in the late 1980's indicate that over 35,000 gay American men go through alcoholism treatment centers in the United States alone per year, and the overwhelming majority of these men are referred to Alcoholics Anonymous upon discharge as part of their lifelong recovery program. In addition, thousands of other gay men enter Alcoholics Anonymous without ever having gone through formal treatment programs. So many gay men are now in A.A., that I recently overheard a gay man joking to a friend that if you can't find gay men around town, go to A.A. as that's where they all are.

Part of the strength of A.A. lies in the fact that all of the members share their stories with each other. These stories generally disclose what life was like before sobriety, what happened to lead the person into sobriety, and what life is like in sobriety. The stories not only show newcomers that they are not unique, but they serve as beacons of hope to still-suffering alcoholics, alcoholics who may believe they are beyond hope.

The stories in this book follow the typical A.A. story: What it was like, what happened, and what it is like now. Each story was written by a gay man of Alcoholics Anonymous who had achieved at least one year of sobriety. These stories are similar to other alcoholics' stories in that they show tragedy before sobriety and joy in sobriety. But unlike typical A.A. stories, most discuss the gay dimension of recovery.

The gay dimension of recovery is critical. In two recent research studies conducted by this editor, internalized homophobia, or seeing being gay as a negative aspect of self, was identified as the culprit leading to alcoholism in gay American men. It is not gay bars which lead to the high incidence of alcoholism in gay American men; in fact, most stories in this volume, like the stories in the two research studies, show that gay men typically drink alcoholically long before ever going into a gay bar. A genetic background for alcoholism has also been identified in over 90% of the cases in both studies.

The stories in this volume show that in sobriety, internalized homophobia disappears, especially when gay men are living Alcoholics Anonymous. It has to. For without self-acceptance, sobriety will be most difficult to maintain over time, and serenity will be virtually impossible to achieve. Not all men in this volume have eliminated internalized homophobia entirely. That's okay. Alcoholics Anonymous is not a program of perfection, but rather one of spiritual progress. And all men in this book seek to make progress on their spiritual journey, living one day at a time.

Robert J. Kus
North Liberty, Iowa
1990

1

The Dreamer

I had a nightmare once in which I was riding in the passenger seat of a car being driven at a hundred miles an hour through the streets of the neighborhood where I grew up. The driver was a stranger to me, oblivious to the danger, as we passed the school, the church, and the house where I grew up. I begged him to slow down, but he only smiled with a crooked grin and pushed his foot down on the accelerator. I pleaded with him to stop, to slow down. I asked him who he was, over and over again, but he wouldn't answer.

Familiar places sped past, but I was trapped in this speeding car, a hostage. I began to see that the only way this nightmare would end was when the car crashed and I was dead. As we approached an impossible curve, I turned again to the driver and begged him to stop. In my last, panic-stricken act, I screamed at him,"Who are you?" He turned to me and said, "I'm you."

• • •

I grew up believing there was something wrong with me. Something so shameful that no one could even speak of it. When I learned on the street what my condition was called, I couldn't say the word because it was considered vile and offensive to God.

As a boy, I played alone in an asphalt lot behind an inner city apartment building in Cleveland where I grew up. I lived in a fantasy world, pretending to be the captain of a spaceship with a gang of children as my crew. But, in reality, I didn't mingle with the other children. I felt different and alone and - in my bravest fantasies - special.

There was a lot of arguing at home. Bitter words. Shouting. I can never remember what the words were, but it seemed as if I were the cause of them. I felt that I was at fault because of my condition, which I couldn't identify but I knew was there. I felt as if I were the subject of ridicule, but I didn't know why. I was fearful a lot of the time.

I drank alcohol for the first time at the age of 7. I was curious. I had seen that adults acted differently when they drank. They seemed to be having a better time. When my parents were away, I climbed on top of a tall kitchen stool and carefully took a bottle of whiskey from the top of a cupboard. I poured it into a shot glass and drank it down. It burned my throat and tasted bitter, but after awhile I felt giddy. The feeling passed. When my parents came home, I hurried to tell them what I had done because I felt that my intoxication showed, and I wanted them to know why I was acting differently. Nothing was made of the incident.

One night, my father fell over on me, accidentally. He had been drinking, but nothing was said of it. I tried to put the incident out of my mind because I wanted to spare my father embarrassment.

I didn't feel as if I fit in at school. I was ill at ease among the other children. I learned that, if I said comical things, people would like me and would overlook the fact that there was something wrong with me.

On one sunny Sunday afternoon, my father was sitting at the kitchen table, drinking with one of his buddies. They were talking louder than they needed to talk. They were more expansive and emotional in their actions. My father was never emotional except when he was drinking with his buddies. He made a point of bringing up my report card, showing it to his buddy. He was proud of me! Father had never said this to me, but he was saying it to his buddy. I knew then that if I worked at being intelligent, my father would be proud of me. If I were smart, my father and my father's friends would overlook the fact that there was something wrong wih me. I vowed to myself that I would be smart.

In high school, I felt awkward and lonely, but I hid my feelings by being smart, by staying in the background, by gaining attention for my good grades and then keeping out of sight. I dated girls because I wanted to grow up and get married like normal people. I thought when I found the right girl she would make me forget that there was something wrong with me, or that I'd be able to hide it better. But boys attracted me. I was curious to know how they acted, what they did, so that I wouldn't feel so different. Nevertheless, I shied away from team sports because I knew I was different and not like the others. There was something wrong with me. It was a secret I had to keep.

When I went away to college, I met other boys who had been praised for their intelligence. I felt more at ease with myself then. It was okay to be intelligent. I felt more normal than I ever had growing up. Not that I was normal, but that I felt more normal.

I had unspeakable desires to be close to other young men. I craved intimacy with them, but I hid my feelings because I believed they were wrong. I knew that if I told anyone of these feelings, I would be ostracized. So I learned to be a "best friend" without ever confiding anything too personal about myself.

Sometimes I searched for other young men late at night off the campus. I met them and had sex with them. It was hurried and impersonal. But it brought out - just for a moment - strong feelings in myself that I had never known existed. I didn't think about getting to know any of these young men better. When the act was over, I wanted to forget it ever happened. I wanted to marry a woman and be like everyone else.

I got drunk and had intercourse with a woman for the first time. Afterward, I felt as powerful as a bull. I knew then that sex with a woman was something I could do, and so I'd got that over with. I was glad I'd gotten it over with. I'd proved I could do it, and I was glad it was done.

When I finished college and got my first professional job, I was struck with an emotional windfall that I'd never experienced before. Never before had I so much free time. I always had had studies to get through, and had worked at part-time jobs to pay my tuition. But now there was nothing to do after work. I didn't know how to play. I dated women, but I felt relieved when I left them at the end of a date. I was lonely. Sometimes I drank whiskey and 7-Up when I was alone because it made me feel better.

I toyed with the idea of going into a gay bar, just to see what went on there. I was away from home and family and school and the "best friends" I had met in college, who by then had "best girls" and wives. My first evening on a bar stool in a gay bar frightened me, but I eased up after a few drinks, and I learned to smile, though at no one in particular. I began to like going to the gay bar. It was the only place where I didn't have to guard my feelings, and I felt at ease once I had had a few drinks.

I met men and, in my private moments, I prayed with terrific intensity that I would meet a man who would make me feel better about there being something wrong with me. I hoped a man would so lighten up my vision of myself that I would begin to feel it was okay to be myself. What I found was that, after I had had a few drinks, I would feel that maybe I wasn't so bad after all. And I'd laugh to myself and feel a little cocky.

I learned how to pick up men. I learned what to say and what not to say, and I learned quick one-liners. I learned to play the game. But sometimes I'd wake up in the morning next to a guy I didn't like at all, and I'd get discouraged. I thought I was getting cynical as I was getting older, but I figured that was normal. I felt tired. People at work asked me what I did in my spare time, and I would make up little lies about hobbies and sports. I'd turn down invitations to go places with people from work. I figured I was different from them, and I wanted to keep my distance. I knew there was something wrong with me but thought I was learning to accept it. I believed that I didn't care what other people thought. When I went to the gay bar, I felt better.

I considered doing volunteer work or getting into a social club, but gave up the idea as being a waste of time. How was I going to meet another guy like myself, if I didn't hang out where gay guys hung out? Who needs to do sports and be in good shape, if you're going to end up sleeping alone until you're dead anyway?

I was starting always to feel lousy in the morning. My

hands began to tremble at lunch time. My memory was getting shorter. My interest in work had diminished. Nothing was working out the way I'd planned.

There was a documentary on alcoholism on public TV one Saturday afternoon. I was curious to watch it because I thought I knew some guys who drank too much, guys I had met at the bar. I poured myself a drink and watched the show. It confirmed my suspicions that some guys drank too much and reminded me that I would have to keep an eye out for that, because I didn't want to become like them.

As months passed, I realized I was missing work more often with the flu or because of tricks who didn't know when to go home. I wasn't eating balanced meals because I didn't have much of an appetite. What I wasn't failing to do was to be at the bar by eleven. One day, my hands were shaking so badly, and my head hurt so bad, that I thought what I had was worse than a hangover; I told myself I'd see a doctor if it got worse. A couple of beers made me feel better, so I figured I didn't need to see a doctor yet.

I was beginning to think I had a drinking problem. Not that I was an alcoholic, but that I had a drinking problem. I figured I would call A.A. and ask for their advice, since they were professionals and probably could offer some helpful hints. A guy came to the house and talked to me about The Program. The guy kept calling it The Program. I hated hearing this. I didn't want to be part of any "program" because I knew that I was different, and that A.A. wouldn't understand. I decided not to call A.A. anymore.

But, a week later, I called the guy in A.A. again; and, then, again, two weeks after that when I'd had too much to drink and couldn't sleep and couldn't stop drinking. The guy said he knew a hospital where you could go and stay for a short while. They would make you feel better, and it was all confidential; you just had to be off work a couple of days. I agreed to go there because I couldn't go to work in the condition I was in. I couldn't sober up and I couldn't get high anymore, no matter how much I drank, and I couldn't even sleep.

While the guy was on his way over to take me to the hospital, I killed off a pint of vodka to calm my nerves. I don't remember going into the hospital, but I woke up two days later and it hit me that I was taking off from work and that my employer didn't know where I was. So I panicked, and I said I had to go home right away. But the staff talked me into staying. They said if I went home right away, I'd get drunk again. I figured they had that pegged right, so I agreed to stay until I didn't feel like having a drink, and then I'd go home.

I filled out a psychological form that asked me my sexual orientation. I wrote down "same sex" because my mind was fogged up. I figured that they were professionals and that if there were something wrong with me they wouldn't tell anyone, because it was confidential. But at the group session, in front of everyone, the counselor asked me, "Are you bisexual?" I froze. I had to be honest in the group, so I said, "Yes." Now everybody knew there was something wrong with me.

I spent the rest of my days in the hospital, keeping quiet and dodging questions about myself. I figured I'd learn what I could about my drinking and let it go at that. I figured that it was nobody's business about the rest and that they should leave me alone. At night I would sweat and my mind would race. I was afraid of what they would do to me now that they all knew there was something wrong with me. I cried to myself.

After I left the hospital, I stayed sober for awhile, but then I went back to the bar and started drinking again. I knew that if I could find a lover, I wouldn't have to drink anymore, or that even if I did drink, I'd have someone to help me though the rough spots.

I met a guy who wanted to be my lover, so he moved in with me. I told him that I wanted to stay off booze, but I needed help. My lover promised to help me. But I hated to feel like a failure, so I hid my beer supply all over the house so I wouldn't have to drink in front of him. I blew the game when I passed out on the kitchen floor, and my lover and some paramedics revived me. I promised to stop, over and over again, but I didn't. Finally, I agreed to go into a treatment center again.

For the first week in the treatment center, I didn't say anything to anybody. I begged my lover to take me home. Nothing mattered to me anymore, I realized. I was just one of those drunks who would never recover; I just wished life would be over faster.

It didn't matter anymore that there was something wrong with me. It didn't matter anymore that I had a lover. All that mattered was that I wished I could die, but I hadn't been able to, yet. It seemed to me that all I did was to go on living and hurting all the time, and I was tired of living and hurting.

People asked me what was wrong with me, and, because it didn't matter anymore, I would say that I was gay. They would say, "What's wrong with being gay?" Those jerks were asking me what was wrong with being gay! As if there were nothing wrong with it! As if there were nothing wrong with me!

I told them what was wrong with being gay: I didn't like myself. I didn't like being gay. I felt like a stranger to my family and to everybody around me all my life.

They said it sounded like as good an excuse as any to get drunk.

"How could they say that?", I felt like screaming. They couldn't know! They don't know!

"You haven't told us what it's like," they said. "That's why we don't know."

So now it was my fault. My fault, keeping it to myself about being gay. Now they didn't seem to care about my being gay. They only seemed to care about my getting drunk. I didn't know what to think anymore. I slept a lot.

When I got out of the treatment program, my lover moved out. I was sorry to see my lover go, but we didn't have anything to keep us together anymore. I didn't need a caretaker, and my lover missed the drunk he used to take care of, to be needed by.

I felt lonely, but I liked having time to myself. I went

to meetings, and I listened, but I didn't say much. I'd read A.A. literature when I hurt inside, and sometimes it helped, and sometimes it didn't. I'd go to meetings, and sometimes it helped, and sometimes it didn't. But I didn't drink.

I liked to be alone, a little bit. I liked to sit in the bathtub and feel what it felt like not to be reeling from alcohol in my system all the time. I liked the feel of hot bath water. I put bubble bath in the water, even though it seemed like a girlish thing to do, because I liked to watch the bubbles. A voice would say to me, "There's something wrong with putting bubbles in the bath water. You must be a sissy queen." And I would smile to myself and say, "Then I'm a sissy queen. But there's nothing wrong with me."

I didn't know how to feel about this new notion that there was nothing wrong with me. It wasn't as if a weight had been lifted off me; there was no surge of relief. I didn't know how to react to such unqualified, unprecedented good news. All my life, every solitary boost to my self esteem had been measured against the overwhelming certainty that there was something seriously wrong with me, something that negated anything good in my favor.

I didn't fight this new affirmation; I just didn't know what to do with it. So I started to play: "What if...?" What if I were okay? What if there were nothing wrong with me? How would I treat myself?

And I decided to treat myself kindly. To reward myself now and then. To respect my feelings and my needs. To forgive my shortcomings. I started to devote less time to the negative messages I had been pummeling myself with when I believed that there was something wrong with me.

It feels funny. I haven't outwardly manifested any miraculous recovery. Nor have I thrown off the bandages and found myself able to walk for the first time, or able to see things I've never seen, or able to leap tall buildings in a single bound.

No. Unlike the hero in a TV movie, sometimes I just stand around, puzzled. The world around me is still the same, but I'm different. Now I'm sober, but it doesn't show in a very visible way.

Only I know how far I've come, and even I don't know how far I am now able to go. I'm alive, and I'm sober, and I am gay. What happens next?

There comes the realization that I have lived my life as a victim. That was yesterday. Today I realize that I can't expect everything suddenly to become easy now that I've found out that there's nothing wrong with me. I'm moving in an entirely new sphere of reference. So I move cautiously, exploring this new world very tenderly.

• • •

I have a dream in which I am driving a new car through the streets of the neighborhood where I grew up. I am the driver. I carry no passengers, no hostages from the past, and I am moving at a steady pace, with my foot controlling the accelerator and my hand guiding the wheel. The school and the church no longer tower over me. The house I grew up in is not where I am living today.

I am leaving the old neighborhood to see what lies beyond it. My vision is clear now and my hands are steady. My heart quickens at the feel of this new vehicle I'm moving in. I welcome the feeling of power without wanting to abuse it. I'm grateful for the feel of solid ground under the car and I welcome the journey I've started.

2

AA Fundamentalist

Recently, a man to whom I'd given my phone number a few months before called me. He wanted to let me know that he was back in the States after having been out of the country for several weeks. Even though he'd not gone to any meetings, he had stayed sober. I hadn't realized he had been away, nor had I noticed that he'd not been at meetings for awhile. I asked him if he'd like to go with me to a meeting the next night. He replied that he wasn't sure if he would be going back to the meetings at all. I then found myself sharing with him a few of the adages I'd heard early in my sobriety. "A.A. meetings are like the premiums we pay for car insurance; we hope we never have to collect from them, but we are awfully glad they are there when we need them." "The least successful way for anyone to stay sober is alone; the most successful way is with others who are not drinking one day at a time." "The Steps of A.A. are what sober folks use to guarantee the joys of living a sober life."

He said that I was probably right, but that I sounded rather like a fundamentalist. I just chuckled and told him thanks! But the man's call prompted me to look back on my life before the A.A. fundamentals became important to me and before I became an A.A. member, and to compare it with the way I live now.

I was born and raised in Rockford, Illinois, coming from a middle-class working family background. Alcohol was a problem in our family from my earliest memory, since my father's drinking caused us many problems. However, my first memory of a distinct personal "drinking problem" is stealing a fifth of Scotch from an uncle's home when I was 17. I attended a Catholic boys' high school. We went on a three day senior trip to Springfield, Illinois. That bottle of booze made me much more popular among my classmates than I had been before. This early episode had two important elements which stayed with me through my 13 years of alcoholic drinking: first, the feeling of belonging alcohol gave me and, second, stealing or something else illegal was often involved in my drinking difficulties.

When in college, I drank with the "pros." I became a regular at a local tavern, fitting in quite well with the drunks. There was an M.D. who lost his privileges of practicing at hospitals because of drug addiction; an overweight coin collector who came in every afternoon, stayed until she got drunk, then went home to her dogs; and a gay, retired serviceman from the Air Force with whom I had my first and only experience as a hustler. There were also the two owners of the bar. I could walk from my dorm to the tavern where I knew I could escape the collegiate concerns of sports and girls. I could be accepted as one of the regulars by real friends, ones about whom I new a lot, but whom I would not have to tell much about myself.

Now about my hustling experiences. To say I was sexually naive is as much an understatement as saying Liberace was just a little bit flamboyant! You get the idea? The retired Air Force man began asking me in 1965 if I'd "go out" alone with him. I sort of knew, but didn't really know, what was involved in "going out" with him. I was excited, fascinated, and interested while at the same time frightened, disgusted, and embarrassed by the possibility. I was 18 or 19 and he was in his 40's. Finally, one night when I was semi-drunk, I went with him to a motel. He gave me $20 for about an hour of the evening. That was almost double the spending money I'd get in the mail every week from my mother. I continued to go out with him once or twice a month until I was graduated. The pattern which developed here was the connection between the necessity for drinking in order to engage in sexual activity.

Prior to graduation, I had two firm job offers to choose between. One was as a management trainee position for Western Electric, and the other was as a high school English teacher. The teaching job paid $5,200 per year and the other $7,800. I decided on the teaching job for two reasons. Our involvement in Viet Nam was just building up, and I could keep my draft deferred status as a teacher. Also, I knew that at Western Electric I'd be expected to be in many social situations where drinking was a necessary part of the business ritual, and I didn't trust myself to be able to handle those potentially dangerous situations very well. At 21 years of age, I already, deep down, knew I had problems controlling my drinking. Nine more years were necessary before I'd admit I was powerless over alcohol, and that my life had become unmanageable.

While teaching, my drinking quantity and frequency began to progress. I also again returned to stealing, but only while drinking and on the "installment plan." I had the combination to a safe where cash was kept, and for over a year I would take $50 or $100 installments. In the beginning of my third year of teaching, I had a one-car accident at 2 a.m. while driving home from a bar drunk. That abruptly ended my teaching career with an arrest for a DWI (driving while intoxicated) citation and the discovery that same night of my theft of some $1,200. I was offered the option of being fired or of resigning. I accepted the latter offer.

My first bout with depression and drinking set in during the fall and winter of 1969. I moved back to live with my mother. I looked for, but couldn't find, a job that suited me. I did, however, find Rockford's one and only gay bar, where I moved back into the familiar role of being a regular within a few weeks. Then I wrote checks on a closed account from a different city for spending and drinking money. My Mom bailed me out when the collectors came and threatened me with jail.

My theatrical career began at that time, too. I got hired at a newly formed dinner theater, as a jack-of-all-trades. I managed the box office, built scenery, acted, stage managed, slept with the resident director, drank, and got fired all within three months.

The bugle sounded reveille, and I woke up to find myself inducted into the U.S. Army as a private. Picture a 25

year old heavy drinking, heavy smoking, totally unathlet-
ic, closeted, immature man thrown into basic training with
mostly 18 year olds. Needless to say, being drafted was a
major trauma. Along with the physical demands, which I
barely met, there was nowhere to get a drink for the first
month. But we alcoholics, like booze itself, are cunning,
baffling, and good at trying to be powerful. On my first
weekend pass, I checked into a motel right outside the
gates of Fort Campbell, Kentucky, and got drunk.

After completing my training, I spent one year in Germany, rising very quickly to the rank of sergeant. I regularly had drinking and money troubles, not to mention men
troubles. While a soldier, I had my first lover, an American
teacher for children of the U.S. Military. He and I drank,
fought, loved, and hated with passion. He wanted to settle
down and make a home, while I was still coming out (really!) and wanted to have a lover and to play around. While
being a soldier, I managed to get my second arrest for
drunk driving. I'd borrowed my lover's car to take a potential trick out drinking, and I ran into a tree on the way
home. I suffered a broken sternum as well as a fatal frac-
ture in the relationship with my lover. It ended when I ran
off to Vienna for a week's affair with a mad Russian lan-
guage-expert who was my lover's best friend!

I'd arranged for a job as a civilian working for the
Army to begin immediately after my (honorable!) discharge. I moved three times in that first year, until I settled
into a very good administrative position in January, 1973.
My drinking now was on a daily basis, and I got drunk
about once a week. I'd learned how to cruise in German,
as I'd become fluent in that language, but that brought me
a very close brush with death. One night, while drunk, I
picked up two hustlers and brought them to my apartment. After a drink, those two "nice boys" stripped me,
bound me, and beat my head with a hammer. They left me
for dead, stole the few pieces of jewelry I had, and my car.
I miraculously survived the beating, both physically and
professionally. My boss, an Army colonel, did not accept
my offered resignation, but helped me to stay on the job.

He encouraged me to use that experience as a means of personal growth. (Years later, by the way, I found out he had a gay son!)

That brush with death, though, didn't suggest to me that I should quit drinking. It did confirm for me, however, that it was truly dumb to pick up two people at a time.

I talked to an alcohol counselor after that event who suggested I check the book Alcoholics Anonymous out of the library, since his copies were loaned out. I was to report to him again in two weeks. At that second meeting, I told him I'd read the book and had not found anything in it that applied to me. Both were lies; I'd been afraid to read the book.

Shortly after that, I became involved with a German man who eventually became my lover. Our relationship lasted off and on for seven years. But when it began, we had two very prominent mutual interests - booze and sex. I depended upon him, most unhealthily I know today, to make me feel superior and, hence, okay. We were drunk by noon every Saturday and had a fight by 6 p.m. About this time, I started writing a red capital letter "D" on the calendar every night I got drunk. Since I was writing that "D" two or three times a week, I stopped because the evidence was too conclusive of what I was.

Early in January of 1976, driving home one night after drinking, I was pulled over by the German police for weaving down the road. My German was quite fluent, and I was quick to anger the police with my arrogant accusations. In Germany, a person is given a choice of whether or not to voluntarily allow blood to be drawn for a blood alcohol test. If a person doesn't consent, the police make a written record of that, then forcibly restrain the person, until the blood is taken. After my blood was involuntarily taken, my car was impounded and I was driven home.

The very next morning, feeling terribly hung over, I met the alcohol counselor while I was walking to report the prior night's experience to my boss. The counselor said I looked awful and asked if he could help in any way. I explained the details of my arrest the previous night. I remember distinctly his very simple reply: "Why don't you give A.A. a try?"

On the evening of January 16, 1976, I attended my first A.A. meeting. It was held in the lounge of an American church. Six men and one woman were there when I so timidly walked in. Since there was a newcomer, all seven of them related something about how they'd gotten to that room and about why they were there that night. After everyone had spoken, I was asked if I'd like to say anything before they closed the meeting. Just before speaking, I remember saying silently, "Please, God, don't let me lie to myself anymore." I told them I thought I might be an alcoholic, might need help, and hoped they could teach me how to not get too drunk anymore. I was offered, and accepted, a white chip to carry around in my pocket, indicating my desire to surrender. (Had they told me to what I was surrendering, I doubt I'd have taken it!)

Two guys gave me their home phone numbers and said I should give them a call. They didn't tell me why, and I found that rather strange. I was shown the Big Book, and it was suggested that I buy one and read it. So that Monday at my first meeting, I accepted another recommendation and bought the book.

The next day, Tuesday, the counselor called me to see how I was doing. He said he didn't want anything else. "Strange, these alcoholics," I remember thinking at the time. By Thursday I'd read several chapters of that Big Book and told one of the guys that I guessed I was just about ready to do the 4th Step, make a moral inventory of myself. He told me that would probably not be a good idea so soon and that I should wait awhile. Strangely, I accepted that advice, too.

During the first six or seven months, I went regularly to that Monday night meeting - and didn't drink. The U.S. Government had already revoked my driver's license for one year, when I received my punishment from the German court system. It was a fine equal to one month's pay! (Germany has a fine system by which regardless of an individual's salary, the punishment for certain offenses places the same hardship on all guilty parties.) I think I bought a new roof on the city court house. Sometime in late summer, I was able to fit a second meeting a week into my schedule on Saturday nights. These were the only two English meetings each week in our town.

In October, I asked a man, who'd become my sponsor (even though we never used that word to describe our relationship), whether we could talk about anything. Overcoming much fear, I told him I was gay. Mind you, several times he'd been in my one bedroom apartment that I semi-shared with my German "friend." It didn't take too much to figure out what was going on between us, but I was still terribly afraid of rejection. I'd spent many evenings with him and his wife and children, and I felt somewhat part of their family. Much to my surprise, he shared with me, a month later, that he'd allowed himself to be picked up often by men for sex when he'd been drinking. He'd not done that for over a year and a half since he'd been sober. I began to be afraid of him and feared our relationship would become sexual. It was a confusing situation for me. He had helped me so much to work on acknowledging and accepting my alcoholism, to start to rely on a power greater than myself, and to begin to make that decision to turn my will and my life over to a God as I understood Him.

Within months, we ended up in bed. I was not able to handle our having a sexual relationship very well. Imagine, in my first year of sobriety, having a lover and an affair with my sponsor, while trying to work on becoming sober, joyous, and free. I was a disaster waiting to happen.

An article in the *A.A. Grapevine* titled "Condemned to life an underground life" appeared in July, 1976, in which the author wrote about his being gay. After sleeping with my sponsor several times and becoming more confused, I wrote to the *A.A. Grapevine* and asked them to forward my letter to the author of the gay article. A reply from the author arrived and simply stated that if I wanted to have an affair with my sponsor, I should do two things. First, get another sponsor; and second, stop beating myself up over it. I tried to do both.

Sometime during that first year I also did my first Fourth Step and took my Fifth Step with a Catholic priest. With my list in hand, I explained to him the purpose of the visit. He listened patiently and calmly. At the deepest, darkest, most embarrassing of incidents, he told me not to carry the guilt around any longer because what I had done was not really a big deal. My, how I awaited the relief that Step Five promises. I so wanted to be able to walk among my fellow humans with my head held high, unashamed and unembarrassed. It didn't work that way for me, or rather only slowly, after much other work to clear away heaped up layers of past garbage. Then I came to experience feelings of placid recovery I now know as serenity.

I was really one of the "sicker than others" when I came to the A.A. program. For years I was convinced that I would live perpetually with anxiety attacks - not the miniseries variety, but the long duration, extended wear kind. Professional help was needed, and I began my first therapy sessions early in my second year of sobriety. My therapist helped me to start to accept all my human qualities - strengths, weaknesses, and indifferent characteristics. During this phase, I worked hard on Steps 6 and 7.

From the contact with the author of the *A.A. Grapevine* article, I found out about a gay round-up in San Francisco. Arrangements were made for me to attend "Living Sober 1977." I arrived in the gay capital of the world never having even met another sober gay person. The culture shock was severe. I found myself afraid and wanting to be alone. These were such common feelings that I'd lived with most of my life; now I was slowly able to recognize and overcome them. How fortunate I was to have had such a great introduction to gay groups of A.A.

I learned how to take a positive inventory during that first time in San Francisco, a tool which has remained in my A.A. kit. I also carried a Step 8 and 9 list with me to my hometown, where I went to visit right after the round-up. The reactions of people to my being in recovery ranged from full acceptance and congratulations, to curt replies similar to, "It's about time you took care of this."

The maintenance Steps of 10, 11, and 12 slowly worked their way into my program. I was privileged to be involved early on in the service structure of the English-speaking European A.A. I held every position, including Conference delegate and group G.S.R. (general service representative). My fundamental grounding in A.A. also included a heavy dose of the Traditions of A.A. One meeting that I went to regularly from about my second year of sobriety on was a "12 and 12" meeting. Each Monday, a chapter about either a single Step or a Tradition was read from the book *Twelve Steps and Twelve Traditions* and discussed.

I moved from Europe to the Washington, D.C. area over six years ago. I now attend a mixture of gay and non-gay A.A. meetings. Both are important parts of my program. I'm fortunate to sponsor both gay and non-gay persons, and I think it worth a few chuckles to be considered by some to be an A.A. "fundamentalist."

With the many benefits of the A.A. way of life, I'm happy with me most of the time. The anxiety attacks almost never occur and, when they do, they only last for a few hours at most. I don't steal anymore, and I usually feel comfortable in most social situations. My goal in life is to be sober, happy, and useful, and I know that I have the rest of my life to complete recovery.

3

The Drama Queen

I was born in 1933 on a farm near Buffalo, N.Y., the last of four sons. My parents were Baptists, Republicans and farmers. Both were college graduates, and my mother had taught school before she married my father. My father, whom I've no reason to suspect was an alcoholic, died when I was four. My mother, a member of W.C.T.U. (The Women's Christian Temperance Union), died when I was sixteen.

I knew when I was nine years old that I like "doing it" with the paper boy, who was fourteen. And I knew I was gay (though I didn't know that term) long before I suspected, let alone accepted, that I was alcoholic. In fact, I rarely drank alcohol until I was about twenty-three and in the U.S. Army, although I'd been going to gay bars since I was nineteen.

At thirty-one, when I started teaching at Michigan State University, I was drinking and getting drunk regularly. Why? The only answer I can give is that I was, and still am, an alcoholic. By thirty-one, I'd completed three degrees (B.A., M.A., Ph.D.), had spent two years in the army, had taught two years at the University of West Virginia and two more at George Washington University, and was delighted to have been hired by M.S.U. Why, then, the drinking and getting drunk? Again, the only answer I can give is that I am an alcoholic; I got drunk because I wanted to.

I'd had only one long affair, which lasted about three years. I was desolate (drama queen that I am) when it ended, but alcohol hadn't been the issue in the break-up. My lover's passion simply had cooled for me. Of course, during the years we were together and especially afterward, I had engaged in a great deal of drinking at gay bars and gay parties. In the '60's and '70's, those were the places where gay people met each other. But I was also doing a great deal of drinking at bars and parties that weren't gay. It wasn't until after I'd been sober for some time that I realized that most of the people at the bars and parties (gay or not) hadn't been drinking nearly as much as I.

The first time I drove home from a bar, parked my car, got up to my apartment, got undressed and into bed, and then couldn't remember any of it the next morning (because I'd obviously blacked-out) scared me...but not enough to scare me into seeking help. There were also times when I'd wake up in the morning, look at the person next to me in bed, and think: Christ, was I drink last night! It wasn't long before the inevitable happened. One morning, the person next to me in bed woke up, looked at me, and said, "Christ, was I drunk last night!" Ah! The romance of two drunks going to bed together! Toward the end of my drinking, I decided that it made more sense - it was easier and cheaper - to drink at home. How's that for clear thinking!

Between 1968 and 1978, I spent six summers in Europe and one summer in the Orient. Occasionally, people would ask me about good places for shopping in Europe. I couldn't tell them anything about that, but I could certainly tell them good places to drink. And I urged everyone to go to Hong Kong; booze was really cheap there!

In 1972 in London, I met a German who was a professor of law at the University of Zurich, Switzerland. That was the beginning of my second long affair. Although the Gnome of Zurich (as I called him) was concerned about and critical of my drinking, distance was a conciliatory factory in our relationship; he lived in Switzerland, and I lived in Michigan. During the six to eight weeks we were together each year (sometimes in Switzerland, sometimes in Michigan), I was able to control my drinking, or so I thought.

By the mid-70's, friends were also expressing concern about and being critical of my drinking. It's not that I became violent or went through a drastic personality change when I got drunk. The scenes I caused were the result of my getting shrill, incoherent, and passing out - in that order. It didn't at all offend me when friends urged me to do something about my drinking. I assured them (and I really believe it) that my drinking wasn't really a problem. They knew I was lying. I didn't.

In the summer of 1978, in Zurich, I realized that I no longer loved the Gnome and that he felt the same about me. So I went to Paris (once a drama queen, always a drama queen) to figure out what I should do. What I did was to stay drunk. Those ten days in Paris were nearly a total blackout. At some point I thought about going to Rome. Lots of good drinking places in Rome! But - amazingly, incredibly - I figured out that, as long as I was going to stay drunk, it would be cheaper to do it in East Lansing than in Rome. So I flew home.

I still had a job, bank account, and some friends. Being gay didn't offend my non-gay friends, but passing out offended all my friends. Many of them (gay and non-gay) made it quite clear that they no longer cared to see me. I was rarely, if ever, pleasant company. I finally realized that I was in immediate danger of losing those things most important to me: my job, my financial security and my friends. Furthermore, I could no longer tolerate - physically or emotionally - staying drunk.

That's what my life was like. This is what happened to it.

One week after I'd returned to East Lansing, I entered the Alcoholic Treatment Program at St. Lawrence Hospital. Although I was drunk when I made the decision, and drunk when I was admitted, by that point I knew that I didn't want to go on being drunk. It wasn't until I'd been in A.A. for some time that I began to realized how totally unmanageable my life had become.

After I'd been in treatment for about three days, I was given the name and phone number of Doug, a man I'd never heard of. I phoned Doug (my brain still awash in alcohol) and told him my name and where I was. He said he'd come to see me that evening. Well, thought I, how pleasant to meet someone new.

After Doug and I had talked for awhile, I said that I didn't understand why I'd been told to phone him.

"Because," Doug said, "I'm gay too."

"Oh,...." was my somewhat tentative reply. It was at that point that I began "to get" the A.A. program.

A.A. was central to the treatment program at St. Lawrence. My reactions to A.A. were, alternately, hostility or indifference. "One day at a time...Easy does it...Keep it simple...Higher Power...Spiritual Program..." Boring, superficial platitudes! Simplistic nonsense! Of course, A.A. was fine for those who needed it. I just wanted to get sober (more clear thinking on my part). Because of Doug, I began to realize that not only did I need A.A., but I also wanted it. And I still do - both need it and want it.

One of the first A.A. meetings I went to after leaving St. Lawrence was a men's group, which prides itself on being hard-assed about hard-love. (It didn't take long to realize that they're a bunch of hard-assed, hard-loving and hard-on-sobriety cream-puffs). At that first meeting I thought it was essential to tell the group that I'm gay.

Sitting next to me was someone named Red. I didn't know it at the time, but Red was notorious for being hard-assed and not particularly gentle with his hard-love. Red leaned toward me, put his hand on my knee, and said, "George, we don't give a shit who you fuck so long as you stay sober." And that was that. Several months later, I asked Red to do my Fifth Step with me. While I was telling him my deepest secrets about my shameless and outrageous life, Red yawned and said, "Cut the nonsense and get to the serious things." And that's what hard-assed, hard-love is all about.

What's it been like since? Just great! Well, not always great. The hills haven't come alive with the sound of music, and I've yet to hear any larks learning how to pray. I still must work for a living and meet the responsibilities of my job. I still must pay my taxes. What's great is that I can work, that I have and can keep a job, and that my taxes are paid. Miracles? Maybe. However, the A.A. program works, and I'm grateful that it does.

In September, 1981, I flew to Japan to begin two years of teaching at Mie University in Tsu, Japan. It was the first time I'd crossed an ocean while sober. Between September 1981 and September 1983, I saw Japan, Hong Kong and Singapore as though for the first time. (I'd been in those places in 1970 but had been drunk most of that time.) I also visited Korea and Russia and an entire continent, Australia, where I'd never had a drink. And for the first time out of four times there, I was sober in London.

Before I left East Lansing in 1981, I had written to and heard from two Americans in A.A. who were living near Mie University: one in Nagoya, the other in Kobe. Shortly after I arrived in Tsu, I was invited to a weekend (the first of many) in Kobe. The meeting in Nagoya became my "home group." Before the end of September, I'd met and became friends with the A.A. people at the Tokyo Tower Group.

Being in A.A. is better than having an American Express card - and cheaper. I've been met at airports, taken to meetings, and given guided tours by A.A. members in Korea, Hong Kong, Australia and Singapore (and I just missed a meeting of A.A. at the U.S. embassy in Moscow).

The only gay A.A. meetings I've attended, except for Australia, have been in the States. But not for one moment do I believe that going only to gay A.A. meetings will keep me sober. Having said that, I must add this: I'm again at Mie University. The Americans in A.A. who were in Kobe and Nagoya have returned to the States, and the Nagoya meeting no longer exists. The closest A.A. meetings to Tsu are in Osaka (two and a half hours away) and in Tokyo (three hours away). But I have a telephone, a typewriter, and A.A. friends who also have and use both. "Meetings" can be on the phone or in a letter.

Something else about what my life in sobriety is like is that in February 1983, I met Michihiro. (After all, being sober doesn't mean being celibate.) He visited me in East Lansing in 1984 and again in 1985. He is a major reason why I returned to Japan in 1986.

When we met, Michihiro had never heard of A.A.

But he has come to accept and totally to support my commitment to A.A. When we were first getting to know each other, Michihiro was convinced that all my friends were gay A.A. members. He's since realized that's hardly the case; many of my friends are neither gay nor alcoholics. All of them, however, like me much more now than when I was a drunk.

I am gay, and I am an alcoholic. But I want to be perfectly clear that, at least in my own case, I'm not one because of being the other. Indeed, I came to terms with being long before I was aware of being an alcoholic. What's more, I can't explain why I'm both. Nor can I explain why I'm right-handed. The simple facts about me are that I'm in love with a man who loves me; I'm alcoholic, but I don't drink; I write with my right hand instead of my left; and I'm having one hell of a happy life!

4

The Dentist

"Did they tell you at treatment why you drank?" was the question my wife kept asking on the last evening I was to ever see her after I had completed alcoholism treatment. My answer was consistently the same, "No, I don't know why, and I may never know. The important thing is that I am alcoholic, and I'm trying to do something about it." That was in my fourth month of sobriety in 1971, and since then I have had continuous sobriety. With recall, honesty, and advances in alcoholism knowledge, the "whys" of my alcoholism puzzle have pretty well fallen into place.

I am the youngest of three children, and I was raised in a small Midwestern town. My dad was one of three doctors in town, and so we kids were under more scrutiny than most other kids - or so I thought. The messages I got as a kid were that I was no better than any other kid, but that I had better get A's and B's, and be angelic in behavior. (When I discussed these perceptions with my folks a few years ago, they were amazed that I had formed them.) Growing up, I felt totally boxed in by these perceived restrictions and obligations. They created much frustration, paranoia, guilt, and fear for me.

I was a Depression baby, and as a teenager in the 40's and 50's I went to many movies. I received the message loud and clear that success was partying at the Top of the Waldorf, complete with furs, jewels, cigarettes, and martinis! Going downtown to the movies was an education in another respect as well. The neighbor boy taught me the joys of masturbation and other sexual activities at the movies or behind the downtown buildings. When his interest waned by senior year, I had become the aggressor because I liked what he and other men had; I still do. But, like my alcoholism, there were many years of denial in between.

My siblings were six and eight years older than I, and I felt saddled with two sets of parents. My folks did not drink, and my mother thought that having a drink was very evil (she still does). She got this attitude from her parents and the troubles she had witnessed in the lives of her father's four siblings, three of whom were "drunks," as she calls them (though she distinguishes me as an alcoholic). So a probable genetic line was there for my generation.

I was on such a tight leash that I didn't do much dating until my senior year of high school. When I did date, I was scared to death of contracting some mysterious venereal disease, and the possibility loomed large of losing out on college for getting some gal pregnant. During high school and two years at a liberal arts college, I probably had no more than 10 or 12 drinks. On our senior skip days into Chicago, our class ordered martinis and Manhattans with dinner. Most of my classmates didn't like them (I didn't either), but one girl and I went around the table drinking the leftovers in the glasses as the others left. She isn't alcoholic - I am.

Everything came together, the physical, psychological, and spiritual aspects of alcoholism in November of my freshman year in dental school. I was temporarily living at my social fraternity house, and after a Big Ten football game, they had a kegger. I studied fairly late, after which I got a glass and a pitcher of beer and began drinking with determination. I had never done this before, and I made up for lost time!

The next Saturday was a big dance and, with no date, I studied until about 11 p.m. when I was asked to tend bar for an hour. Behind me there were shelves of booze I had never tasted. I was bombed in an hour. It was a repeat of the week before - getting drunk, sick, and passing out. I believe I became an alcoholic on those two Saturday nights.

Over Christmas vacation, I got a room downtown. The pressure of school was really hitting me; I was afraid of flunking out and had insomnia. I decided to arrange my study schedule so that I could go to the bars and have a beer to help me sleep. In retrospect, in a period of six months, four signs of alcoholism were present: (1) I put a high priority on alcohol despite being in academic trouble; (2) I never sipped that beer - I gulped it; (3) not then, nor at any time in my drinking career, could I ever stop with just one drink; and, (4) I was using alcohol as a medicine. My genetic/biochemical predisposition had "kicked in" early on.

I progressed through dental school satisfactorily, but the quantity and frequency of my drinking increased. With the knowledge we have today, I could have been diagnosed alcoholic when I got my D.D.S. Although I was fairly well liked all my life, self-doubts that I was truly accepted persisted, despite the drinking camaraderie. I was seen as a "good party boy who sometimes drank a little too much." By this time I was in love with a nursing student, and sexual thoughts of men, despite enjoying looking at them, were denied and repressed.

Upon graduation, I went on active duty as a military dental officer. I discovered the great affordability and access to booze. By now the layers of alcoholism denial were complete. I was the son of a doctor, a shining light in my community; I was now a doctor myself and laden with the brass and braid of an officer. In each of the communities I lived, a common assumption prevailed: no doctor was ever an alcoholic, and no doctor, if he had a successful practice, ever treated "those kind of people." (Unfortunately, much of that attitude still prevails today.) With all the layers of denial insulating me from the truth, the most I admitted was that I drank too much sometimes (nearly daily), but certainly I was not a drunk. That big D - Denial - nearly cost me my dual career - dentistry and the military. So, I made a jackass out of myself all over the world, and it was to be 17 years before any dental colleague or boss was to confront me about my alcoholism! Talk about enabling! Of course, in the 60's, few knew that a way existed to arrest this disease. For the military, no officer was a drunk - except that they did tolerate, frequently rotate duty assignments of, and, in desperation, boot out "incompetents." The trouble was that most were highly skilled and intelligent personnel - when sober.

Over the years, in forays into cities such as New York City or Los Angeles, I would get what few lavender publications were available then - the nudist publications or photo magazines of Adonises in jockstraps or briefs. But I was straight...

I met my wife-to-be in August at the Delaware beaches, and we were married in December. She was a good-looking, sharp woman, and marriage was the thing to do - a career enhancer; after all, I was moving up the ranks and was 30 years old. She was a pretty good drinker and seemed to enjoy sex before we were married. But she called me an alcoholic on our honeymoon, and she would hardly drink or make love from then on. Was I glad that I kept porno pictures from Hong Kong, for they and my right hand kept steady company for years. I told myself that the women in the photos were beautiful, but I always stared at the generous and gorgeous hard male endowments! At an A.A. meeting, I once heard a man say he couldn't remember making love to his wife without booze. That seems to have been my case, too. Vodka had become a more reliable lover for me.

By the late 60's, the dental corps pretty well knew I had a problem. Now the junior officer did the dentistry because my hands had become tremulous. I was a mass of sweat - changing clothes many times a day. I smelled of booze (my wife said "exuded") from my breath, skin, and lungs. My skin itched all over. My paranoia was getting such that I decided it was better to drink at the Officers' Club than not, for the officers wouldn't talk about me if I were sitting among them. I also had to find out what I had done the night before, because I was always passing out. I have passed out and slept in some of the strangest places around the world. One bartender even made me a seat belt for my bar stool! Yes, I was a normal social drinker. Many times I've thought about when I first knew alcohol was a problem in my life, and surely I knew way back in dental school.

I had several car wrecks in the early 60's - one became a dreadful lawsuit that came to trial in my third month of sobriety. In 1970, I was overseas, alone, and after an evening of martinis and no food, I sideswiped four taxicabs. This was the beginning of the end.

When I came back to the States, I reported for duty on Friday morning, had a vodka lunch, and blacked out in my car outside the main gate. I was put in the military hospital to dry out and was supposed to go to work on Monday morning. I refused to be released and demanded a complete physical exam. That was my cry for help. For two weeks they conducted many tests on me during the daytime, and I got drunk every evening. The binge culminated in my driving in another blackout and going the wrong way on a one-way street on the base. The powers took a dim view of that behavior, and I was restricted to the hospital.

The next morning, the hospital administrative officer came to my bed and told me I was being processed for a general court-martial! As sick and mentally confused as I was, I understood being hit by a two-by-four. A 13 year dental and military career was down the tubes.

For those days during my hospital confinement (1971), I had a savvy red-headed no-nonsense Irish nurse who would come into my room every two hours. No one else came in during her shift. She would get me talking, then go to the door of the room and say, "Do you think your problems have anything to do with you drinking, Doctor?" and duck out before I could make my denials. After a couple of days, the common denominator to all my living problems was getting obvious - even to me - alcohol. I was proceeding to surrender the idea that I was a social drinker and admit that I was an alcoholic.

She hit me up to go an A.A. meeting. Of course, it wasn't my cup of tea (or vodka or anything else), but with a threatened court-martial hanging over my head, it seemed wise to go.

I was taken by a retired officer, and it was a grim meeting. No one smiled or laughed; I have avoided those kind of people and A.A. meetings ever since. Despite that, I did identify myself as an alcoholic that night - it was a bit of a shock to me, too. I went back to my room and thought about the experience until about 4 a.m. I pondered such important things as how I could eat pizza without having beer! I then had two large vodkas on the rocks, decided I was truly alcoholic, and went to bed. By the grace of God, alcoholism treatment, and Alcoholics Anonymous, that was the last alcohol I have ever used.

An old aviator boss came to my rescue, saying I was too good a guy and too good a dentist to get booted out. It was difficult in 1971 - there were just a handful of treatment centers then, and not well known. But after 30 days of sobriety, I was headed for 75 days of treatment. Yes, I was a sickie, but the military was also eager to get a military officer sober.

I was now in southern California and remained there for my next tour of duty. After nine months into sobriety, it became obvious that I would have to choose between trying to patch up a bad marriage or keep my sobriety. I had firmly believed (and still do) that sobriety is life, and sobriety is the number one priority in my life. So, divorce proceedings were started.

In doing my A.A. steps, I didn't get into sexuality issues - I assumed I was straight. I knew the marriage was doomed, and my second most important priority was to get seven more years of military duty in for retirement. In my first months of sobriety, I met another recovering alcoholic dentist - and he was gay. I really wanted to be more friendly with him, but I was scared of screwing up my shaky future, and I was also afraid he might talk. Instead, I started going to Hollywood about once a month to buy gay magazines, and, after carefully casing the area, I got nerve enough to start attending gay movies. Though I was practically afraid to look cross-eyed at anyone there, it was physically and emotionally gratifying knowing that there were quite a number of men interested in men. During this time, I dated a young woman who used sex as I had used alcohol, but she taught me that sex was fun, clean, and okay. At age 39, it was pretty late for me to be learning that, but it was a great revelation to me.

Over the next four to five years, I was becoming more
and more concerned about what and who I was sexually.
My sobriety was okay - a few rocks in my path, but I was
growing and enjoying life. I was back to being what I had
always strived for - a damned good dentist, an honest and
respected person, and a credit to my communities. I had
been promoted as a recovering alcoholic, and my goal of
attaining retirement was realistic.

I had now come full circle. I was now known as a recovering alcoholic after so many years of being known as a
drunk. In early sobriety, I felt I had to come to a decision,
an anonymity decision. I had a disease, alcoholism. I was
a doctor, and disease was my business. I felt it was time to
put my money and mouth together and to stop hiding my
recovery. I did not break the A.A. anonymity - just my
personal anonymity, and it was one of the best decisions I
ever made. It relieved me of the guilt and paranoia and of
the same kind of hiding I had done as an active alkie. I
was free, and the decision brought me great peace of
mind. I am sure that it didn't particularly help my career,
but my career was pretty well screwed up anyway.

I went to another duty station for my last four years,
making new friends and dating one woman for a couple of
years. But the sexuality question remained in my mind.
Was I really wanting men, or was it all a fantasy trip?

Eleven years ago I retired at age 44. I tried dating for
another year or so, and found it just didn't seem to make
any difference - when I had sex with a woman, I was
thinking about a man. It was then that I started to have a
few very limited experiences with men - the book store bit
- but I didn't enjoy that. What the hell was I, I thought?
The whole world seemed to have a sexual life and I didn't.

On a trip West, I went to see an old college friend
whom I was sure was gay. We finally got to a sexual dis-
cussion, and I revealed I was confused, that I just didn't
know whether I was straight, bisexual, or gay. He told me
to forget about labels - just do what was natural and enjoyable. He said I might pursue men today, women tomorrow, and men again - and that was okay. Having had

some difficulty accepting the label "alcoholic," it was good to hear that I didn't now have to wear a neon sign with "gay" flashing on my forehead! It fit so well with what I had learned very early in sobriety - do what is comfortable. I have left a cocktail party and a sexual encounter more than once because the vibes were bad.

In my life at the present time, I have combined my profession with my recovery for a new career. It is my version of working the 12th Step of the A.A. program, and it's very rewarding. My recovery program has been applied to working out my sexuality, and slowly I have grown toward self-acceptance. It took three years of sobriety before I could like myself as a person, but it took somewhat longer before I accepted my gay self as something positive.

Gay life is frustrating to me at times. My openness about my recovery scares people away, as does my age, and my less than Adonis' looks. With my relative newness to gay life, I find myself seeking and wanting association with other gay recovering guys, I suppose to reinforce my own self-acceptance and for reassurance and comfort. Living in a smaller city, I have to travel 100 miles one way for gay A.A. meetings, support groups, or bars. And not being a forward person, I find strangers are frequently ignored by the ever-present cliques.

I am not "out" in the usual sense, for I feel it would jeopardize much of my constructive educational efforts of the past eight years. I have received a very high honor in my profession based on my activities as a recovering alcoholic. I see no reason to possibly handicap my future usefulness to my profession.

God has truly blessed me by giving me the tools to pursue a happy and productive life. I thought the world had given me lemons for many years, and perhaps it had. Not only did I have a problem with alcohol, but I had serious living problems, as well. I was the first military officer ever ordered to alcoholism treatment, and many thought that such a program was folly. With help from many sources, I found and maintained sobriety.

Since then, I have come to terms with my being gay,

and the peace of mind I now have is truly fabulous. I wasn't seeking the lemonade I've enjoyed since choosing sobriety and accepting my sexual orientation, but it's great!

5

Taking Off the Lampshade

I was born to a large family on the eastern end of Long Island, New York. I was the youngest child and had my first drunk at the age of two. This was the proud accomplishment of my older siblings who found my swinging around on the trees lining our front yard in drunken abandon rather amusing. I cannot credit myself with getting intoxicated until I was six years old. When six, I snuck into my father's bountiful wine cellar and helped myself to a generous portion of elderberry wine. Fifteen minutes later, I was doing cartwheels on the front lawn and chasing cars while barking on all fours. My mother was mortified by the incident, but then, she is the "sober duckling" of our family.

When I was thirteen, I went to Europe with a group of exchange students. There, free of age restrictions on drinking and the pleading glare of my mother's eyes, I drank. In Italy, on one particular occasion, I got riotously drunk and made numerous passes at the chaperones. Repeatedly, I danced about wearing a lampshade on my head. By the time I had my final drink, I had worn an amazing assortment of such apparel. Since the other students and hotel guests were clearly bored with these antics - as original as I thought they were - I persevered with new jests. These included throwing furniture out of my balcony window and yelling Italian obscenities at the police who subsequently gathered below.

The next morning, I entered the huge conservatory where breakfast was being served to our group and several hundred hotel guests. As if I had come in naked, a great silence fell over the room, and I felt all eyes turn on me. That was a perfect position to be in when I was drunk and wanting attention, but it was a very embarrassing one when I was sober. It seemed like hours before I reached my table and before the chatter slowly resumed. One of the chaperones told me to apologize to the entire room full of people, but I refused.

In high school, I tried other drugs, especially marijuana and acid. The first time I tripped, I told my best friend I wanted to be on acid every day, but as soon as the trips got scary, I abandoned all drugs but alcohol. In fact, I became quite the anti-drug moralist while I escalated my consumption of the liquid drug, alcohol.

After graduating from high school as "class clown," I left for college. There I became an exemplary student by day, leading numerous academic and social organizations and even making it into the annual Who's Who in American Universities and Colleges listing. By night, however, I was the model drunk - inconsiderate, unpredictable, and overbearing. My girlfriend, a Native American studying psychology, finally told me that she would no longer deal with "two" of me. I drank furiously for oblivion after we broke up and was comforted by the young man who had moved in across from my dorm room. He seemed to watch me in the most peculiar way.

This young man became my first male lover, but it was not a liberating relationship. Far from that, for me it was a torrid affair full of guilt, blame, and abuse. I would draw near him and then push away because he was living proof of my own gayness which I felt and feared. And so I lived in dual denial; I denied my sexuality and my alcoholism. I lived in spiritual distress from day to day and from drink to drink.

I felt so desperate one night that I called A.A. and went to a nearby meeting. I wasn't ready to hear the simple solutions offered by the program, so I decided that it was another tour of Europe - not A.A. - that would bring harmony into my life. This final binge led to an arrest in Hungary and expulsion from Salzburg University where I had enrolled for some courses. I indignantly refused to leave mid-semester, so I was given another chance. The Dean had to step over my unconscious body a few more times before I finally left Salzburg.

Back in the States, I returned to the A.A. group I had

once attended on the "mainline" outside of Philadelphia. I was twenty-two and had taken my last drink. I heard old timers in A.A. say that they envied my youthful arrival into the fellowship. This did not console me because I felt like a hundred years old, and I knew that I had woken up on more than my share of crusty stained bed sheets hours and miles away from where I had taken that first drink. Gay sex, like the rest of my life in alcoholism, had been full of disappointment and disaster. No Prince Charmings take drunken clowns home with them.

A hospital meeting linked me up with a temporary sponsor. A service representative told me that this sponsor was a sixty year old priest and that I would meet him that night at the A.A. meeting. I told the representative that there must be some error and that this sponsor placement would prove utterly inappropriate, but she reminded me that it was just temporary, so I went to the meeting that night.

I was surprised when the sponsor walked right up to me as though I were wearing a "Newcomer" sign. I was also surprised when he turned out to be a delightfully wicked man of the cloth. His sense of humor and vibrant personality startled me, and he swore as well as any of the mainline housewives at the meetings.

After a few weeks of meetings, I confessed my gay sins to the good father and promised reform. I told him that I would understand if he felt that he could no longer sponsor me. I shook like a leaf. He grew silent and looked very thoughtful for a few minutes before he turned to me with a broad smile and said, "Don't worry about it, darling!"

Not only did I manage to get hooked up with a gay sponsor, but I also took a new job in physical therapy. After several months working with the most compassionate women I have ever known, my boss confessed that she had been in the program for years! This therapist was also one of the first people I ever told about my homosexuality. After apologizing to her for lying about the "girls" I had said I was dating, I told her the truth. She yawned and said, "Well, that has all the impact of telling me you are Buddhist and not Islamic. But I'm honored by your sharing."

My boss's apathetic response to my being gay taught me that the response of others is not central to the coming out experience. Just as making amends is something we do for ourselves regardless of the outcome, I found that my honesty was its own reward whether it meant that I met acceptance or rejection. Being out as a gay person has been an important process in my recovery from both the demented thinking of alcoholism and the loathful messages of the larger society. Of course, being out is only one way of dealing with one's gay identity; there are many ways, and we must each find our own way at our own pace. Like sobriety, our gay experiences and ideas are individual and change a little each day.

I had some very odd reasons for attending meetings in early sobriety. First of all, I wanted to find out who "John Barleycorn" was. He was in a lot of the literature, and when I asked my sponsor to point him out, he told me to keep coming around. I was also fascinated by the blond wig one woman kept balanced on her head at the "Mustard Seed" meeting. I also went to the Sisters Off the Sauce (S.O.S.) meeting on the mainline where I especially related to the domestic problems they discussed. (After several months, I was told that it was women-only group, but I was still invited to attend until my sobriety seemed stable.)

The Steps were another part of my recovery both early on and presently. During my First Step, my sponsor provided me the "20 Questions" (a test to determine whether one is an alcoholic) to help me accept the fact that I was, indeed, an alcoholic. I answered "no" to having blackouts, arrests, or any hospitalizations due to alcohol, but passed the test anyway. Later on, I answered "yes" to those questions because I found out that "not remembering" was a blackout, that arrests in foreign countries counted, and that I would not have landed in the hospital due to my fingers being cut in a mock sword fight unless I had been very drunk. My denial is not what it once was. It is one more lampshade that I have put down.

I am now sober for seven years and barely remember the awful insecurity and confusion of my drinking days. I have had a second male lover and was able to give and receive in that relationship. A quiet serenity replaces the screams for attention I once had to make. While I still struggle with my defects, I no longer try to be the "A.A. Posterboy" with all the right answers. I have to say "I don't know" before I can even begin to seek answers, and I need to join the sidelines in order to find a sense of belonging. I have had "center stage" jobs as a principal and as a business director in the past, but I found myself to be unhappy in those types of jobs. I have taken other public positions and even served as general chair of my city's Freedom Round-Up, but I still found myself grasping for more attention.

It seems that for me, even in sobriety, I have a philosophy that anything worth doing is worth overdoing. This has led to low self-esteem and backsliding - not to mention a blackbelt in shopping! But sobriety does get better in spite of myself. At least in these sober years, I have never needed to don lampshades. They are always on my lamps.

6

Priest from Down Under

My name is B., and I am a gay alcoholic man. That has been my self-description for the last 14 years. Most of who I am can be understood by those three categories.

I am in my early 40's, am an Australian, and have been a priest for nearly twenty years. Those descriptions are not as significant as my being gay and alcoholic, but they are also important aspects of who I am. I meet with, work with and make my community among all types of people, but my primary community has come to be the fellowship of Alcoholics Anonymous. I'm especially close to the gay A.A. groups. I did not need gay groups of A.A. to get sober, as there were no such groups near where I lived, but my experiences of gay A.A. groups have been very rich indeed.

Being a part of the A.A. community helps me be who I really am; it helps me stay sober, sane and living in the here and now. It was among people like myself that I began to unlearn the distortions and the lies, the hatreds and the fears that a fearful and hateful society had instilled in me about being gay. It was among A.A. people, and especially among gay A.A. men, that I began to understand how I had cooperated in my own oppression and deprivation. I learned that staying sober and sane means accepting the person God made me to be.

My personal experiences, both before and after A.A. entered my life, tell me so many things about the world and about myself. I grew up in a rural environment in Australia. Later I lived in Chicago for a couple of years and found gay A.A. groups for the first time. After two years of study and work, I returned to Australia and to the isolated rural environment. I had been a member of A.A. for twelve years before I came across my first gay A.A. group. I sometimes think that the Higher Power may have worked it all out beforehand, because after my contact with gay groups in America, I was able to begin to really integrate the two most important components of my life: being alcoholic and being gay. That integration has been years in the making. But the happy and healthy acceptance of these parts of my identity have really only just begun. The struggle for personal integration and self-acceptance is the story of my life up to the present; it is the lens through which I have come to know and to value who I am. My encounter with my being alcoholic and gay was the real beginning of my coming to a deep and personal experience of a God who understands me.

Growing up in rural Australia during the 40's and 50's was not exciting or even interesting. It was just life, and there were certain basic truths by which we lived. These truths were sometimes articulated by the local church or by the local township. The most important truths were not articulated at all; they were just implied and absorbed. These were some of the more basic assumptions: blacks, or the Australian aboriginal people, were little better than animals and didn't really want equality; women should be either virgins or mothers; drunks were the lowest forms of life and morally degenerate; and gay men, pejoratively called "poofters" in Australia, were lower than the lowest since homosexuality was against nature itself!

Obviously, growing up to be alcoholic and gay were the furthest things from my desire and intent when I was young.

My father was a farmer. When I was growing up, the people I knew well were farmers, priests, and housewives. Business people, merchants, physicians, and professional people were around, but it was assumed that I could not really aspire to be like them. My future felt mapped out for me. I would become a priest or farmer. From early adolescence, I had serious thoughts about becoming a priest.

A facet of my self that I buried from any conscious awareness was my sexual orientation. I became aware of being attracted to males as early as six years of age. I can still remember a vivid highly erotic dream featuring naked males when I was six or seven. Actually, I never thought this attraction to males was anything unusual, even as a teen. But around age eighteen, to my dismay, I learned that very few men felt as I did. I had innocently assumed that all men were like me! I had no idea whom people were talking about when spouting hatred towards "poofters" and "queers." Then I knew; they were talking about people like me. Well they would be wrong. I would not feel the way I felt; I would banish these feelings whenever they surfaced. And that is what I did.

By this time I was attending theological college, the perfect world in which to bury myself and my embarrassing emotions. That is what happened for six or seven years. I did this so well that when friends spoke about the difficulties they were having with sexual feelings and thoughts, I thought they must be weak. After all, I rarely had any thoughts in that direction. I was attracted to Michelangelo's "David" and other classical works of male subjects, but that was art, not sex. I also was attracted to anthropology, particularly the books featuring naked hunters and gatherers. After all, priesthood candidates were supposed to broaden their education!

Of course attractions were always there, but they were disguised and hidden. So it continued - my studying for the ministry, denying my sexuality, and beginning to drink more and to get into trouble with alcohol. As these late adolescent and young adult years passed, I developed a reputation among the students for being able to drink everyone else under the table. Unfortunately, this skill was unreliable, and sometimes when drinking, I would get suddenly sick, drunk, disorderly, or all three. When I drank, the world became brighter; the colors, more vivid; the sounds, clearer; and my emotions became anything I wanted them to be.

I encountered all the other experiences a young person goes through: separation from parents, developing a sense of unique identity, gaining a foothold in the world around me, and acquiring skills that would equip one for a productive life. As a child, I had quickly developed an appreciation of what was appropriate, sane, and holy, and what was definitely inappropriate, possibly insane and indisputably unholy. In the rather rigidly defined social and religious world in which I lived, such recognition of, and conformity to, the accepted norms of identity and behavior were necessary, if I were to survive in that world. There were no alternative ways presented, so I accepted this socialization process without questioning it.

After being ordained a priest, I was sent to a country town to minister. I was confident in my new role as priest, but not quite so confident within myself. In my new role, I was particularly drawn to the world of the poor and alienated, especially the Aboriginal people. Inspired by their struggles to overcome the harsh and unjust definitions society placed upon them, I tried to become part of their world, at least in a small way.

My drinking became steadily worse, and people tried to alert me to the dangers. I met their efforts with hostility or puzzled hurt. This steady decline and the denial could have gone on for years, but I was thrown into a major crisis, falling in love with a middle aged gardener.

In my part of the world, well brought up young clergymen did not fall for men, and never for gardeners, but I did. We were both startled by our love. My friend especially was quite unnerved by falling for a young priest, but he soon got accustomed to the idea just as I did. So began the most wonderful, loving, and disastrous relationship I could imagine. I became obsessed with him. Instead of beginning the relationship with each gradually sharing his life, we immediately began to merge our lives. Although disastrous, it did lead me to accept certain realities about myself, namely, that I was gay, terribly burdened, and had buried my feelings for years. It was as if my sexuality and my inner needs were finally emerging.

This affair lasted a number of years, with little sexual activity but enormous emotional confusion for us both. We alternatively loved and hated each other, and we were always dangerously dependant on each other. My friend worried about my drinking and outrageous behavior when drinking. I was obsessive and possessive about him.

A major crisis was in full flight. My drinking changed, over a period of no more than a month, from heavy to chronic daily drinking. I would stay intoxicated weeks at time.

I won't go into a lengthy "drunkalog", but merely list some of the typical things that happened to me. Total loss of control around alcohol became the characteristic way I lived. I got drunk when I least expected to, and I got sick on any and every occasion. Repeatedly, I got lost. I would lose my car regularly, forget where I was going, and often would wake up ignorant of the day, date or time. My parish work deteriorated so much that I was embarrassed to stand up in the pulpit on Sundays. I increasingly withdrew from family and friends. I came to care for only two things: my lover relationship, and where my next drink was coming from.

Alcoholic denial became so entrenched that I remember declaring to my local superior one day that all my troubles would make sense if I were an alcoholic, but that since I wasn't, I must be going mad! Logically, everything pointed to alcoholism, but nowhere in my conscious mind could I see any connection between it and me. I even got professional counseling. I told the psychologist my whole life story, except for the bits about my drinking and love life. Not surprisingly, the counseling was useless. It never occurred to me that dishonesty would not help things.

Finally, I was near the point that I could not count on remaining in the ministry. I was determined to hang on to what I had for as long as I could, for the ministry offered me three things: protection from the damage my troubles would inflict; guarantees of a home and food; and money for alcohol.

As shocking as it may sound, I had no lofty or noble reasons for clinging to my ministry. Ideals, inspiration, devotion, prayer, and work among people were all values that proved to be soluble in alcohol.

The final months of my drinking were quite painful, and I rarely think of them. I do remember, though, the pain, shame, ultimate isolation, and despair. My daily life consisted of finding another drink, staying out of people's way, keeping my friend close by, and, then, finding another drink. At times I escaped to Sydney or Brisbane by getting three weeks to a month of sick leave so I could give all my attention to alcohol. But I was still obsessed with the relationship with the gardener, so I would worry constantly about him while gone.

On these sick leaves, I would disappear into the flop houses and cheap wine saloons where my money would last longer. I had by now given up rum, whiskey, vodka, and other spirits. Instead, I combined cheap wine and metho. Metho, which is quite toxic, is popular with derelicts and homeless alcoholics and is actually methylolated spirits, a type of wood alcohol. I knew of its toxicity, but it was cheap and effective. Finally, the idea of suicide crossed my mind. It seemed a preferable alternative to living this way, but my fear of pain and my sense of shame at what people would say about me when I died prevented me from killing myself. Amazing as it seems, the denial was still in place, so I used many rationalizations about my drinking.

The turning point for me came with a statement by a since-deceased acquaintance of mine, a homeless Aboriginal and chronic alcoholic man named Harvey. Harvey and a friend lived under a bridge on the edge of town. One day Harvey was trying to get drinking money from me, but I wouldn't part with it. I needed every penny for my own drinking. Abusing me loudly on the street, Harvey said, "How dare you refuse me money for drink. You're an alcoholic like me; if you keep drinking, in a few months you'll be living under the bridge like me." His words stung me; they shook me at my core. Harvey's words had more credibility than any I had heard in several years, for he was a professional alcoholic. From that moment, I knew that I was in the final stages of chronic alcoholism. I could see that I had only a few months left before irreversible damage, both physical and psychological, would begin to appear. I was at a crossroad: one way led to recovery and a new life; the other way led to more of what I had been experiencing. I chose the road to recovery.

Back home, I went to see to see a woman whom I knew to be in A.A. Staying with her at the time were several old timers from the early days of A.A. in Australia. They all set to work on me immediately. I began to feel understood and accepted. Before encountering these people, only my friend had approached me with such easy intimacy. Here were five people who sensed who I was, what I was feeling, and they accepted me. Their love began my relationship with Alcoholics Anonymous.

I began to attend meetings in that rural Australian town. Being a priest, I was well known, but that made little difference to these people. To them, I was just another drunk trying to make it back to real living. Their care was genuine and offered to me, not pushed on me.

Almost immediately, I hit a snag. After a couple of weeks, I was beginning to feel physically human again and saw that the program did work for these people. I could not even read at the time, so the Twelve Steps were unintelligible to me, but I intuited that if I did what the members suggested, I need not drink again. This was a fearful and happy thought. I knew I wanted to be well, but I wasn't sure if I wanted to be free from alcohol. It took me nearly four years to make up my mind, which is why I always think of my rock bottom lasting four years. Physically and emotionally, the worst part was before coming into A.A. But the spiritual issues and the identity crisis caused me to remain in an often traumatic limbo for those nearly four years.

In my early A.A. days, I used simple cliches to stay sober. Two that I used frequently were: "I can do for one day what would appall me if I had to do it for the rest of my life" and "Keep it simple." The Serenity Prayer began to serve as a life raft for me. I kept sober, one day at a time.

Those early months in A.A. were very formative because I felt this is where I belonged. I felt I could not talk too freely because the A.A. meeting was, I presumed, composed of only straight people; and I, of course, was gay, a priest, and involved with a local man. But the most important things in my life just then were staying free of alcohol for one day at a time and beginning to live again. The local group could meet most of my basic needs as a recovering person who was just beginning the journey.

Eight months into sobriety, I drank again after experiencing a crisis about my friend. Another dynamic leading to the relapse was my indecisiveness about whether I wanted to be permanently free from alcohol. The drinking episode, although lasting only a few days, had dreadful results. Not only did I get terribly ill, I messed up a friend's house, caused havoc with his family, and frightened the neighbor's children. Embarrassed, I sobered up and began again.

I got back into A.A., but several months later, I drank again. This time, I drank for three months with dreadful results. Surprisingly, I had continued my A.A. contact during the second relapse as I knew the lifeline was there if I wanted it. This second episode so damaged me that I ended up being ordered by my superior, physician, and the police to enter a treatment center. Despite serious fears and reservations, I went in and for three weeks loved the company, A.A. meetings, therapy, and staff. These people challenged and even shocked me. After my physical and psychosocial evaluation, the verdict was that I had a lot to lose and had just about blown my last chance of recovery. This was the shock that challenged me to take action.

When home again, I requested a transfer to another town. This was part of my effort to begin to change or end the obsessive relationship with my friend. I was transferred and became especially close to the Aboriginal people.

For the next three years, I was mostly sober with occasional drinking episodes that lasted a day or two. In these three years, I never left A.A., but I continued to wrestle with the question: Did I want to be free from alcohol? Beneath this question were the issues of who I was, who I had become, and, ultimately, what was my truth. The Twelve Step program kept telling me that if I wanted peace and sobriety, honest use of the steps would help. This I attempted, but nothing really worked. I found I could neither pray nor share myself openly with others because my deepest personal concern, my gay orientation, was forbidden territory.

This point in my life was my real rock bottom. The earlier trauma of living a near death-like existence had propelled me into a program of recovery. The anxiety that now tortured me arose from my continuing reluctance to begin using the program as it was written, though I clearly recognized how imperative it was for my well-being to do so. This internal conflict was, in a word, Hell.

I had ended my relationship with my friend well, and a genuine mutual friendship developed. We are still good friends. This left me to deal only with my own internal personal issues and with certain social justice concerns.

My life among the poor, especially the Aboriginal people, had radicalized me to the injustice and oppression that underlay not only Australia, but the whole of western society. So, social concerns became my personal concerns, too. But my church people were conservative rural people, and my perception of social reality sounded like fighting words to them. Many, maybe even most, of my parishioners were racist and quite hostile to black, Asian, or gay people. My being with friends with Aboriginal people somewhat alienated me from many parishioners, but not all of them.

I was still undecided about total abstinence, but I did use the program on a daily basis and kept sober most of the time. The decision to take on the program, in fact to accept life itself, actually happened quietly and gently. I knew that being honest with God, myself, and one human being was quite beyond me, but perhaps contact with God was not. Formal prayer, where I was face to face with God so to speak, was very threatening. I needed some non-threatening way of approaching God and the spiritual dimension, a "back door" approach.

I had practiced various forms of meditation years before, so I decided to return to one of these called mantra meditation. It simply involved putting myself in the presence of the divine, while using a simple word to center my attention. Over a period of months, I began to change, and the change, I believe, has become permanent. What the change meant - and means - is that I have not had a drink or mind-altering drug since that time. When the fight and struggle went out of me, I began to hand my life over to a power greater than myself.

Since that time, my life has radically changed, and the promises of the A.A. program have begun to fulfill themselves in my life. Beginning to meet God and the spiritual dimension within myself is really what the Eleventh Step means to me. The remarkable thing is that by giving up conscious control, I gained a new life and gained real control for the first time in years and began to move into freedom.

For four years I had been trying to "do it my way" in A.A. Finally, I said, "Okay, God. Okay, A.A. Okay, life. Have it your way. I'm ready to try living on your terms, but only for one day." There was now a basic difference in the "one day at a time" approach. Before handing over my life to my Higher Power, I had used this "one-day-at-a-time" approach to consciously be free of alcohol for one day, but now I was using it to be free to live for one day, and to live on life's terms, not according to my controlling or compulsive version of life. I was beginning to do what is called the Third Step, though at first I did not recognize this.

I began to observe how I functioned, what my concerns and issues were, and how I reacted and behaved in general. I was beginning to more intimately explore my own inner life, which is the principle behind the Fourth Step in A.A. What was happening was similar to the process described in the first three steps of A.A. I had no trouble identifying myself as powerless over alcohol or that my life had become unmanageable. I could accept that my inner conflict regularly led me to insanity. And I was now actually beginning to ask God for help and to open myself up to life.

The whole process was contained in the simple act of handing over my life to the larger picture, or God/cosmos, and the smaller picture, or my inner self. I had resisted this step for years because, in my mind, it was the equivalent of giving up my independence, my will, and my own unique identity. But, as I persisted in my daily mission of handing over my life and will, a genuine inner strength began to emerge, my sense of personal dignity and unique identity became stronger, and my own freedom truly began for the first time. It is a paradox - giving up the fight wins the battle, surrendering your will gives you control, and opening up to the ultimate empowers and nurtures your personal identity.

During these four years, I had kept my gay identity secret from everyone except my occasional sex partners. I was beginning to suspect, however, that what I had learned about homosexuality and same-sex sexual behavior from my family, society, and the church were not accurate. My own experience and understanding of who I was kept growing and challenging these acquired beliefs. I began to hear contrary voices within myself. The strong voice said I was intrinsically bent, warped, or sinful. The smaller, weaker voice told me that being gay was not only good, but also holy and vital.

At the end of my fourth year of limbo, I realized I had to share my own reality with another person. I knew the value of sharing oneself from A.A., but my A.A. sharing, even with my sponsor, was limited to safe issues. I needed to share more deeply.

I finally chose a priest friend of mine to do a Fifth Step with. Bearing my soul to him became the most liberating experience I'd had in years. Saying the words, "I am a gay man" nearly choked me, but they freed me. He listened carefully, said little, and I knew he respected what was happening. It was a most liberating experience.

My first years of alcoholic recovery had been plagued with relapses. These ceased to occur after I had taken my Fifth Step and admitted I was gay. Telling another human being that I was gay unleashed the power to stay sober and to grow and develop as a person. Living a lie, no matter how sanctioned, only leads to self-destruction.

Today my life is very different from the four years of struggle and pain. I needed those four painful years, however, to learn how not to live life. Today, I can relax and just live as the Author of life intended.

I find it difficult to articulate how liberating this opening up to life was. It set in motion a chain reaction that continues today, more than ten years later. I had been well defended against the world, but publicly engaging in it easily - as paradoxical as that may sound. My best defense against hostility and threats from people was to win them over by interacting with them as peers, or as people I understood. I was gregarious and found it easy to do. The catch was that in trying to relate as one of them, I often found myself compromising my own moral beliefs and acting out roles that were inconsistent with, or even contradictory to, the self that I really was. Sometimes I was an accomplice in my own oppression. Instances of this were common enough when I was young. People would be telling anti-gay jokes, and I would smile weakly, rather than protest and risk attracting hostile attention. I chose to protect myself from verbal ridicule. But the conflict this provoked between the truth of my inner reality and the role of conforming to the public's expectation of manly behavior that I felt compelled to play was actually life threatening. Alcohol and, indeed, any chemical or behavior that put a buffer between me and life when it was like this was a welcomed relief to me. But this actually reinforced the deadly gap between my inner truth and my outward performance. The process of healthy change took time. Willful control of my life and of others would often battle with the more successful handing over to life's energies. But the more I chose to hand over my will and life to the Higher Power, the more real choice, actual freedom, and genuine living all began to emerge. What I experienced was a resurrection of life's energies.

I became very heavily involved with a rehabilitation center that worked mainly within the Aboriginal community. This really helped me share with others what I had found to be true and healthy through A.A. I could identify with these people in many ways. They, too, were alienated from the mainstream of society; they, too, had seen their reality defined by others; they, too, were stereotyped by people at large, and they, too, absorbed all this and often turned it on themselves. But I could never feel free enough to tell them that I could share their experiences because I was gay. And being white and a priest made this reality invisible to them.

Often I would not let myself feel the alienation and oppression I experienced as a gay man. But as I grew in A.A., the instances of conflicting feelings and conflicting beliefs about being gay increased also. I, too, had absorbed all the lies, hatreds, stereotypes, and definitions that church and society had thrown at me; we were unhealthy, unholy, and a threat to normal society. Increasingly, however, I was beginning to see that my inner reality, and that of my gay brothers and lesbian sisters, was not as we had been brought up to believe. Still, a part of me felt it to be wrong. Conflict!

I then began more seriously to question the church and society's positions with regard to being gay and to other social issues as well. This process had the effect of pushing me away from both the bosom of the church and the hearth of society. Bosoms and hearths were not for the likes of me! But did this reflect the mind of God? Was my basic reality viewed in this way by its Creator? Before answering this question, I had to search and analyze the circumstances under which I lived.

Imagine my situation: a closeted gay priest ministering in a rural Australian town, who was a member of a regular A.A. group, and who was a friend of the Aboriginal community and of many other people whom society had pushed to the side. I was both hated and admired. I had many supporters in the local church and among the wider community, but I had at least as many non-supporters. I was respected, even loved, by most of the Aboriginal people. And here I was, questioning the description of my basic personal nature that both church and society had given me.

I developed physical symptoms from the conflict and related stress in my life, symptoms such as stomach ulcers and tension headaches. I understood the sources of the conflicts and the causes of my physical ailments, but I could see no way out of my situation. I was in regular contact with God, using meditation and, by now, more formal types of prayer. I was still convinced of the basic goodness of the church, of my role as a priest and of my work. To hear my inner personal truth described as a disorder and a basic evil had one of two effects on me; either I repressed my feelings and felt nothing, or I felt enraged and even violated. The irony is, that while I was maturing in my sobriety, I was deteriorating emotionally and physically because of this inner conflict about my being gay. Often the conflict would go unexperienced for weeks, sometimes for months; then I would find myself separating into two people: "ordinary me" who was a fine young sober priest, and "horny me" who would run after anything in pants.

Despite the unresolved conflict over my sexual orientation, my life of sobriety was a great blessing. I learned to trust in ordinary friendships, and I value friendships above everything. I learned about oppression of various people such as gay men from informal study and travel in various societies.

Over the years, I attained a considerably expanded vision of societies and a much larger appreciation for diversity among cultures. But I was still dichotomized, still split in two about the issue of my homosexuality. The regular contact with A.A. kept me in touch with the strengthening and life affirming power; but it also kept me aware of the conflicts and tensions that are also a part of living.

I became popular among some of the clergy and church people as a spiritual companion, as someone with whom they could talk about and share their deeper personal experiences. I felt rather gratified by this, but wondered if they would still come to me if they knew what I was "really like." This was my attitude, and it showed that deep inside a part of me still believed what church and society had told me about myself; I was unhealthy, unholy, and possibly a danger to society.

I went to Chicago to study and work for a few years. For the first time I was exposed to a gay community. Gay communities existed in the major cities of Australia, but the only time I had had contact with them was to try to pick someone up. I had never sought out gay men who were working out their spirituality and their values in light of their experiences of being gay. But I did this in Chicago, and part of the reason why was that the sheer enormity of the city made it comfortable for me to participate in the gay community in many ways and, yet, to retain my privacy.

Especially important to me was the opportunity to participate in gay A.A. groups. Here I found people who have been through the same experiences as I had and who were working towards an integration of fractured lives and torn psyches. Most importantly for me, I left my experience of gay A.A. groups in Chicago firmly believing that I am not an unhealthy, unholy, or threat-to-society person.

Frankly, it is difficult to understand why society perceives gay men as a threat. Perhaps it because people fear that more and more gay men will adopt a spiritual way of life like that found in A.A. Perhaps a society that defines us as unhealthy or bad or bent feels threatened by us because more and more of us no longer experience ourselves as the way we are defined. Perhaps the perceived threat is to the narrow definitions of loving sexual expression that our churches allow, especially when we gay men know that God has intentionally made us as we are.

I have seriously studied both psychology and scripture in recent years, and what I have learned confirms the experiences of fellow recovering gay alcoholics. I have found insupportable the ecclesiastical and societal use of both scripture and psychology to condemn the gay reality. I have found insupportable the attempts by both the church and society to justify the condemnation of my inner reality and the oppression of my gay brothers and lesbian sisters. With regard to my scriptural studies, I have found some translators and scholars exceptionally uncritical, or, even worse, mischievous and malicious. To put it mildly, some Biblical scholars intrude their own hidden agenda into their scriptural interpretations. The church's use of such tactics in scriptural translations is even more suspect and prejudiced. Many modern, and not so modern, translations of the Christian scriptures are very inaccurate regarding those passages that address same-sex sexual behavior. Of course, homosexuality, the sexual orientation of gay and lesbian persons, is not addressed in the scriptures at all, nor need it be. The Bible as it exists is sufficient for gay and lesbian Christians to find complete acceptance within the moral system it provides. But rather than rely on the official teachings of the church, I have found that I have had to rely more and more on my own experiences and knowledge of what is true, holy, and just. This can be risky because I have used rationalizations before to avoid the truth. But while I am in contact with the A.A. program and in contact with other gay men who are involved in spiritual and personal growth, I can impartially and critically evaluate my search for truth.

My own inner truth is certainly a reflection of God; this is a tenet of all spiritual traditions. If my inner truth tells me that I can only know peace, wholeness, and inner unity by valuing and appreciating my being gay, then, that is God's call to me.

Where am I then? I am still within the Christian tradition, but choosing to dissent from a particular application of the tradition's ideology. I am in a critical relationship with this tradition, but a relationship nevertheless. The Christian tradition has carried God's word to me and has been the vehicle through which the liberating reality of God reached me. I have to resist identifying the message with the messenger, the vehicle with the reality it carries.

At times I feel I am in a lonely place and, even, in an uncertain place. I cannot rely on my tradition to provide me with descriptions and definitions of my inner reality that bear any resemblance to what I know and experience to be true. But I do need this tradition and the Christian community, even though it sometimes appears that they do not need me. I can do nothing else but accept the liberating God who comes to me, and whom I have found especially present among gay alcoholic men like myself. I unreservedly believe this God has a special liberating purpose for such as us. What function we gay men will serve in the overall plan of the universe, I am not sure. But I do know that our inner sexual identity is not disordered or evil, but is a divine gift given to a minority.

I have life; I know love; I value freedom and experience it's liberation. I can feel the energy that we call sexuality giving me life, responding to life, and bringing growth. I can feel pain and depression now without fear of falling apart. I can know painful memories and share pain and suffering among others, and still give thanks for each day of my life. I have a spirit that is shared by all people, but which I could not know until I accepted myself as a unique and good gift from God. The knowledge of who I am is the first gift that a loving God has given me. Through A.A., and through gay men's struggles for freedom and life, I can now know life itself. There is a unity that I sometimes experience, a unity to the world of things, people, and places. It is a profound unity of all creation with its Creator. Sometimes I can experience this, but only when I value the first gift of the Creator - namely, myself.

7

Return from the Spirit World

"Know thyself." And I do, but not always by choice. I am Chris, and I'm a gay alcoholic....second generation alcoholic, maybe more.

My parents moved from Missouri to Houston in 1942. They had a daughter, Judy, the following year. I came along in 1949, and my brothers (perhaps unexpectedly) in 1955. The first six years of my childhood were problem free. Then I noticed my mother gradually becoming more and more unhappy because my father refused her much independence, such as driving, gardening, painting the house or spending money. He always impulsively said, "No." He was a very conventional male, although he genuinely cared for all of us. Mother developed crippling rheumatoid arthritis and gained weight on her prescribed cortisone. This caused her to increase her drinking. She did learn to drive and also to apologize for her drinking. Neither parent attended my sister's wedding. They did not attend my high school graduation either, but my father did go to my college graduation.

During mother's drinking binges, she would accuse my father of being queer or chasing women. To my knowledge, he did none of those things, but he did argue with her about my upbringing. He felt I should be in sports. I protested but consented, however, to learn to swim, box, and use the bow and arrow at the YMCA. By now I was nearing the sixth grade. I remember many boys that I persuaded to get naked with me, but I remember one in particular, Cliff. His parents let me spend the night while they went out. Cliff and I waited until dark when we stripped, climbed the fence in the back yard, and wrapped the neighbor's yard with toilet paper. We were almost caught

and had to climb a tree to wait before making a safe re-
treat. Once inside, we masturbated together before bed-
time. My rebellion had begun. A case in point: I stole several small items in a hobby shop around this time, but I
felt so guilty that I never repeated this action.

My teachers seemed to like me; however, I did not
really get close to anyone emotionally, even to my friends.
Luckily, I had some good friends with good parents who
always accepted me. Even my mother, obnoxious and embarrassing though she was when drinking, could apologize for her behavior, tell me she loved me, and make me
feel that she really meant it. My father, on the other hand,
rarely complimented but often criticized me. At the time I
didn't perceive his criticism as abuse; he was just as likely
to put himself down. He had loving feelings for me; he just
couldn't communicate these well. I remember when I was
six or seven and being on his lap. He used to "whisker"
me and tickle me affectionately - until he said I had gotten
too big to hold or kiss. Overall, everyone seemed to miss
my childhood.

When I was in junior high, I had terrible headaches. I
was small for my age, was always in the front row of
school pictures, and was last to be chosen for sports in
school. I had some chronic prostatic problems that were
not diagnosed correctly until my late twenties. The size of
my penis was an issue then because we were required to
swim in the indoor pool in the nude, and I was small for
my age and still pre-pubescent in the eighth grade. I was
emotionally immature as well. Girls did not interest me as
much as the boys did. Although I knew the words "homosexual" and "queer," words which were bandied about pejoratively, neither I nor anyone else knew clearly what the
words meant. However, there was lot of sex play without
any satisfactory knowledge of what to do.

My grades suffered greatly in junior high. I acted up in
classes, even in those classes for the very gifted in which I
was enrolled. I sometimes wrote about many of my home
problems. My teachers just said "Too bad" and gave me
A's and B's. I won second place in a regional spelling con-

test when I was recruited as a joke on a Friday by the speech teacher for a meet on the next day; the original entrant was ill. I entered speech and drama where the instructor told everyone that my name sounded like a stripper in Dallas. I wrote a fictional religious biography "Rhadamanthus, The Savior" after reading some of Plato's Dialogues and other philosophy the day Kennedy was shot. Junior high was over!

Once I acquired my driver's license, social activities began. These activities included taking out girls for the purposes of demonstrating my masculinity, for drinking, and for smoking pot. My friends were usually wilder than I was, so I thought nothing of their trying LSD and psilocybin, but it was I who introduced my older sister to marijuana. Increasingly, I spent time with my friends and employer as they drank. On one of my first nights drinking, or trying to, we purchased beer. As we were drinking, one of the guys threw out a Coke bottle into the ditch. A policeman stopped us and took us to jail on possession-by-minors charges. Another time, the police caught us drinking politely in a Czech beer hall; they graciously handcuffed me to a jukebox while rounding up my cohorts. On one New Year's Eve, I got so drunk that I got into a fight with a china cabinet at someone's house.

I did not attend football games at school, get my picture in the yearbook, or go to dances. The night of the prom I drove around with a Greek friend who was enamored of me. The following week, my mother's drinking got so bad that she wrecked the car. She was hospitalized and quit drinking without treatment. Instead of flowers, I bought her an iguana. I finished 237th out of 832 in my senior class and was a National Merit Scholar. So much for high school.

In college I fit in better. It was a commuter college, so on weekends, most of the students went home. For those of us who stayed the weekends, Friday evenings were special. In the afternoons, I would detain the dorm mother in my room for tea, while others would sneak in liquor. After the dorm mother would leave for the evening, we sometimes would stop up the bathroom shower drains and turn on the water till it overflowed into the hall. When we were fairly soused, and the water was flowing faster than the booze, we would get naked, run and slide down the enormously long dorm hall floor. Although I was attracted to many men, I still dated women; and until my senior year, I had not figured out what could be done with men. In time, I became a teacher, and teachers drink on weekends. Jobs were hard to find, then, and Ph.D.'s were shown on the cover of *Time* magazine pumping gas.

I applied to almost a hundred school districts until the semester began, but got no job offers. An employment agency referred me to a psychologist who had developed a new treatment plan for juvenile delinquents, psychopaths, and drug users. The program included a school that was so good that the state licensed it, and probation officers from several states kept it full. This is where I landed a teaching position The staff had to live in and supervise 24 hours a day in this little Texas town. On weekends off, we would rush across the county line to buy beer and then drive into Houston for sex or carousing. Discipline and restrictions at the school increased to my discomfort. I left at the end of the year. Relieved, I went to graduate school for a Master of Education degree. The state subsequently closed the school for abusive treatment of the children and filed murder charges on the owner. He was also accused of homosexual advances toward several students.

At this time, homosexual sex acts in Texas were considered to be sodomy, a felony. Bar raids were common. Since I wanted to be a teacher, this put me into a quandary. Luckily in graduate school, I met an owner of a brokerage house. He offered me a job, so I took my test for licensing as a commodity broker and began a lucrative, if brief, career.

There I learned about wheat and corn, along with a roll in the hay. All the brokers drank excessively and exhibited gamblers' attitudes about their own lives. At a company Christmas party, a black bartender with my name fueled the revelers. After the party, the bartender had no way home, allegedly. Well primed, I offered a ride. In his apartment for another drink for the road, the subject of sex came up. He produced photographs of himself in drag. I got drunker and more willing; I trusted him somehow. We had sex. I was tense despite the liquor, and it was painful but pleasurable at the same time.

At the time I was living with a beautiful, smart, and kind young woman in a commune of sorts, but I didn't feel I needed to be accountable to her for my actions. The two story house we lived in provided us several households. Some of my old students came by, occasionally, without a place to stay. One of my college roommates, Bill, visited once. Karen lived upstairs but more usually slept with me. She became irate that Bill would be staying with me that night. He left; she got drunk and stoned; I got drunk. She slept with me for awhile. She also bit me.

I don't recall the provocation, whether I had snored, thrashed around in my sleep, or done something else, or if she had just aggressively bit me. But the next day she was severely bruised. She moved out that day. One of my male house-mates and his friends (mostly foreign females) frequented gay bars in the area, especially where drag shows appeared. I started going with them, then began to go by myself, At first it was lonely but the glitter kept attracting me back.

Commodity trading was fast burning me out, despite the big bucks I made at it. As an example of how well I was doing, I often bought the household liquor, and it was not uncommon for the six of us to have a $1,200 total wine and liquor expense for the month. I was the only one making any significant money. Their average pay was $600 per month each.

I signed up for the Peace Corps. After a year of waiting for an answer, I decided to take a position as a child welfare protective services worker. After I had bought car and indebted myself to other items, the Peace Corps responded, but I reluctantly had to decline at the time. The child welfare agency had trained me and taught me about transactional analysis and physical abuse. The therapists were famous and seemingly knowledgeable. However, no one that I recall, ever directly asked me about myself or my family in the training, though I was inquiring into my sexuality and my own family's illness, but not too deeply. In the casework, I had much contact with professionals who seemed often to have far worse adjustment problems than I did, frequent divorces, and the like. Daily, we workers had contact and confrontations with hostile parents and with children seeking relief through running away, drinking, or abusing drugs. For our own relief, many of us caseworkers did LSD, MDA (the love drug), and many others. It all seemed good for me then.

On weekends I visited home, now with need of financial assistance. I frequently went out to gay bars and just as frequently got seduced or vice-versa, but not with any real intimacy or resultant affairs. My migraines had been diagnosed. I was treated with tranquilizers and ergatamine tartrate, and told to eliminate extensive driving and stress, and improve my health with a vacation.

The following day, a state holiday, allowed me to sleep late, until I was awakened by a friend on the way to his bank. I accompanied him there, and he suggested we visit some elderly acquaintances to have some screwdrivers and Bloody Marys. We drank for several hours. Then we went to his beach house for lunch and some Scotch. He offered me some white crosses [speed] which I tried. As evening approached, we decided to go into Houston for a steak dinner and to visit a mutual female friend with whom I had lived in the past, and who knew of my sexual orientation and Joe's enabling. She was aware of dysfunctional dynamics, having been one of six daughters in an alcoholic family. We took a gallon of Scotch and a gallon of distilled water along with a bag of ice. When we picked Mary up, we continued to drink, then smoked a joint before deciding where to eat. We chose a fine restaurant.

I could not eat but ordered wine. I began to get rowdy and to put all the table's silverware in my pocket. I felt literally green and was escorted to my car, told to lie down and to take it easy or to sleep while they finished eating. I tried, but soon the speed overcame the alcohol, and I got up and simply drove off. Several miles later, a wave of depression over the relationship with my father and the general failure of my life to be the way I wanted it made me cry. The sadness got worse until I simply decided to drive into the freeway retaining wall. Once the decision was made, my spirit felt a great relief, that is until I hit the wall and the steering wheel crumpled around my head. The last thing I remembered was saying, "Oh, shit! I'm dead!"

I began a trip down a long tunnel with a light at the end. At the end I was met by a being who informed me of my options. I could see beyond into the light and feel incredible peace. I could also hear moaning as, in sadness, spirits were lamenting their past actions, and they were now witnessing the resultant tragedies and outcomes of their actions. This, I was told, was what we thought of as Purgatory; that when we die by suicide we are still aware of earthly events and must watch the effects of our own actions on those left behind. This lasts until the ripples of our actions die out; then we can move into the higher realms. Since I had committed suicide, I could choose to go beyond the light and observe the ramifications of my actions on others or I could return to Earth and finish out my life (as I had circumvented the natural order of things - I had come too early). I could cross over, never to return, or I could go back. The choice was mine alone. However, if I stepped across, I would be forced to watch the results of my behavior on others for a very long time. This was Hell... not a place, but an existence of looking sadly upon failure and continuing tragedy. If I chose to return, my task would be to show others the "Way." No instructions. No more information. I didn't not know if the voice was that of God, Jesus, the Holy Ghost, St. Peter at the Pearly Gates, or just a vivid imagination in a last burst of cerebral activity at the moment of death. Whatever my choice, I was told, I would ultimately return to go beyond the light. I chose to return to be among the living.

Doctors were cutting on me without an anesthetic when I awoke. They did not administer anesthesia in shock cases like mine. My jaw was fractured, ribs were broken, numerous cuts and gouges scarred my body, and my left leg was severely dislocated. They wired my jaw shut and put me in traction. I could see clearly the bed number at the foot of the bed, but nothing else. A nurse gave me morphine, and the day ended.

Many ministers came by to see me, but I refused admittance to them all. The last one was a Methodist, my family's denomination. He offered to pray with me, but I declined his offer, too, on the basis that I was an atheist. He said that all atheists are Christians dying to get out and left.

Doctors told me they might have to fuse my leg permanently in either a sitting or standing position. Which did I prefer? I decided to get better and not make the choice.

I left the hospital after a week in traction and returned home on crutches. Dreams of eating pizza taunted me. However, I could secure nourishment through liquids, choosing first malted milks, then Bloody Marys. My father made them for me. That's where I was. At home.

After four weeks, I returned to work in Galveston, briefly, until I determined that no upward mobility lay ahead in child welfare services. I was now financially strapped, as the insurance did not pay all that I owed on my car, nor did the insurance pay any dental bills. I purchased a new car that I could swivel into and out of easily. Then I quit my job for a bicentennial tour of America. I persuaded an old college roommate to accompany me and, at the same time, to front money for several trades in the commodity markets. We traveled to the East Coast: New York, Philadelphia, and Washington, D.C., staying in cheap motels or YMCA's; my friend, straight and naive, attending all the homosexual haunts of America. It took him 3,000 miles to figure out why so many people had been nice to him.

With difficulty finding a job and the necessity of having one pressing on me , I returned to Texas to work for the state in a crisis unit where, for the most part, I discharged my duties well. I also discovered that social workers as a group have many problems of their own. In documenting cases of abuse, I picked up an interest in photography, which I decided to pursue. No one would hire me as either a writer or a photographer, so I figured I needed to work around professionals of that sort. I decided to work in a retail photo store that specialized in pro equipment, although the pay was low. There I met a good man who spoke of one of his current jobs and the need for a writer/photographer; my new career was launched. I also moved out of my parents' house now that I was 29 years old. I moved in with a group of gay men (all drinkers) and lesbians (who drank even more). We had many fine times, but several difficult ones, too. One time, for example, I was mugged coming out of a notorious leather bar on New Year's Day, knocked unconscious, apparently for my camera, and dragged far enough to wear a large hole in one knee of my Levi's and one in my peacoat. The paramedics revived me but told me they could not transport me home. Without glasses, bruised and dazed, I sought my way home. A passing cab took me to the hospital for free.

Subsequently, I moved several times, as I became disenchanted with my employers. Job after job followed, each promising a lot but delivering little. Finally, creditors started calling every day. Then, I had to go into the hospital for a prostate operation. After admission, the nurse asked me a series of questions for the anesthetist prior to surgery.

"Do you consume any alcohol? One to five drinks?"

"Yes."

"Five to ten?"

"Yes."

"Ten to twenty? Seven days into twenty?"

"Yes"

"Twenty to forty?"

"Yes."

"Seven days times six drinks?"

"Yes"

"Forty to sixty?"

"Yes."

"Sixty to ninety?"

That is six drinks a day for five days (30) and maybe ten or so on a Saturday (40) and how many on beer bust day - "Yes." Then I realized something. I thought perhaps my prostate problems were being aggravated by the activities at the baths, but no one mentioned a concern about my alcohol consumption. I was very promiscuous sexually, but only once could I remember of ever having had sex sober. That was once in 1982; that was what I realized.

My sister came over to my apartment when I got out of the hospital. On Christmas Day we decided to do something different. We rode around and visited friends and drank. We decided I should move in with her now that her children were grown. We were good company. She was straight and understood me well. So it was settled. Shortly after I moved in, she began to have blackouts, then acted strangely. One Saturday night I came home from work while she was burning fried chicken in a rage. We tried to talk but couldn't seem to communicate because I had a sinking, sick feeling inside and she was extremely intoxicated. So I went to a motel with a bottle of wine to get away. She went to the hospital where she later admitted herself for alcoholism. When I found out, I mixed a gin gimlet in relief.

Family therapy four weeks later involved me. My mother refused to go. My brother tried to break sis out of the hospital but was unsuccessful. In therapy, they asked me, "If alcohol has caused you so much grief, why would you ever drink?" That was on August 8, 1983.

Since that date, I have read my way halfway through a small library, published some things on a small scale, returned to my job as a writer and producer of training programs, bought a house, and lost weight. I also had a lover of some fame who was a writer himself, but we eventually ended the relationship. In sobriety I have also dealt with the underlying anger toward my parents, this with the help of a therapist, a gay A.A. group, and all the people I drank with who have also changed their lives. My sister is still a very good and sober friend. I don't go to the baths or engage in promiscuous sex. I have established boundaries and eliminated some "friends" whose behavior would not allow mine. I can love again. I appreciate every morning and every evening. My life is a pleasure.

I believe that my problem is not really alcohol; that is just a symptom. I can't ever drink again, I know that, but my real problem is co-dependency, reacting to outside events in a way that causes me grief and hardship. I am having to change my way of living altogether. With the Adult Children of Alcoholics and the therapist, I have faced some of these issues. My favorite support group, other than my friends, is a gay A.A. group where I find many wonderful people. I am just beginning, after four years of sobriety, to come out to them, not as gay, but as human. I'm finding that I am a very kind and good person who has had some unfortunate childhood experiences, and who has made some poor, decisions based on or influenced by these experiences at a previously unconscious level.

When I look at myself, I see a man who is decent, intelligent, hard-working, honest, and sometimes good-looking to others. My self-esteem has grown but not the ego. My finances are improving along with my health and judgment. I can have fun again. The honesty has relieved the mental pressures and no great traumas have befallen me. I take some pride in my progress, but I take no credit for my achievements. I am lucky. I have no sponsor. No one ever asked me to tell my story before, and I haven't until now. But I know the way, and I hope I've shown it to you.

8

Someone Else Just Like Me

I was born, the oldest of five children, in rural central Michigan nearly thirty-one years ago. In our household my father and mother fought frequently, usually about my father's drinking. Virtually every summer my parents would break up, only to come together again "for the sake of the children."

School life did not offer much peace for me either. I was small and I was frequently harassed. My only means of protection were my brains, which put me in good stead to verbally protect myself against attackers. Nevertheless, I suffered a lot of grief from my classmates' torments.

My early compulsions for baseball and drawing offered me escape from the turmoils I experienced at home and in school. I became quite good at both of these endeavors, just as I became quite good at drinking. My obsession for playing baseball 12 hours a day, 7 days a week, or drawing for nearly as long in the winter, indicate to me that I may have had a compulsive personality from an early age.

I also exhibited "early warning signals" of being gay. Yes, I helped mommy with housework. I was one of the "best little boys in the world." I also had a very close male friend named Greg from whom I learned a lot about life. Greg taught me about all the fun stuff in life: booze, drugs, smoking, and sex with men. Greg was the high school jock and was a B.M.O.C. (big man on campus). However, God gave him good looks and strength to make up for where he shortchanged him in good sense. I tried to provide the latter.

At about 14 years of age, I began to rebel against my parents' rules. This rebellion coincided with learning the lessons on the good life Greg taught me. I began to party frequently. At first I only drank on weekends, but gradually drinking took place whenever I had money.

By the time I was 17 years old, I was drinking enough to get drunk nearly every day. Around this time my mother left my dad for 6 months. I graciously handled my father's money during this period for him. And in so doing, I found I could afford daily drinking.

At age 18, I went off to college - architecture school - at the urging of my mother. Although our family was poor, I had good grades, the Democrats were in power, so I got a free ride in college. Nevertheless, I felt a need to borrow about $20,000 for college while there. This money mostly subsidized my drinking. (Today I receive a healthy reminder of my past behavior once a month when I pay my student loans.)

In college I learned about drinking alone. I soon went from drinking as a festive event, as it had been in high school, to drinking as an escape from the feelings I experienced in college. The pressure to succeed and the desire to be accepted needed to be washed away. As a result, my drinking and drug usage escalated dramatically. The school motto was "Work Hard - Play Hard." I was the Dean's fair haired boy, so I did just that.

As my drinking increased, I justified my excessiveness by the fact that I had some of the best grades in the class. My projects were also getting raves for their creativity. I failed to recognize, at that time, that I was working twice as hard as anyone else to achieve the same results.

I also became an infamous campus legend for my antics while drunk. I was becoming good at acting and saying the unthinkable, whether inebriated or not. I nearly caused a riot on our campus when I openly insulted a bartender's racial heritage and sexual orientation. I took up telling people I had special attributes, such as an ability to read minds. I forgot such ordinary items as bathing, haircuts, shaving, wearing clean clothing, or social etiquette. I began mentally to wander deeper into my own little reality, which I began to fuel regularly with alcohol. Consequently, I didn't have too many friends in college.

One special friendship began to develop, however. Bob and I worked together on a school project, and we grew close in the next year. He took care of me in ways that I needed. Bob made sure I bathed regularly, dressed neatly, and did things besides sit and drink. I, in return, helped him with his school work, as we were in the same classes. We had a true symbiotic relationship for about a year.

One day I decided to get very drunk and tell Bob how I really felt about him. I told him that I loved him. We consummated the relationship during the next two nights. Then Bob didn't speak to me for almost a year.

His "Catholic guilt" was as foreign to me as my alcoholism was to him. My loving Bob seemed a very natural extension of myself. I was aware of homophobia on our campus, but I was already such "bad press" I figured being gay would be just one more weird thing about me.

To deal with Bob's guilt, I chose the vengeance route. No compassion from this alcoholic. I decided I was going to show Bob how much he meant to me by "really" doing some drinking. I see today that I was on a very large "pity pot," and that I was using vengeance to justify my uncontrolled drinking.

Around this same time, my younger brother decided to commit an armed robbery and conspire to commit murder. His trial generated quite a bit of publicity because the murder that my brother, his friend, and his friend's mother committed was of the father of my brother's friend. Our family got to read detailed accounts of our family life in the newspaper and to hear about our family on the radio. My mother attempted suicide. While she was doing this, my father and I sat in the kitchen and sadly recounted our sad fortune to each other as we drank.

Bob's isolation, my brother's trial, and my mother's near suicide left me with ample justification to get drunk. I began to drink in public, oblivious to others and to whom I was with. I began to be publicly intoxicated to the point that I would pass out in public places, such as in parks. I began to get the shakes and hallucinations. I quit eating. I had a car accident. I began to commiserate with some pretty weird people - street bums, psychotics, and panhandlers. I had frequent blackouts, and I began daily to contemplate suicide.

At this time, I began to go to gay bars. I would usually be very drunk by the time I got there. I got thrown out of some bars for passing out once I got inside them. I got thrown out of a lot of restaurants, too, for being loud and belligerent while drunk.

As these events occurred, I began to realize that I was out of control of my drinking. I guess it was when I was contemplating suicide that I realized not everyone went home at night after work and drank till 2 a.m., and that I recognized that I might have a problem. It finally dawned on me one evening that I wasn't going to kill myself after all. My ace in the hole turned out to be a bluff. In my remorse, I called my mother and said those immortal words, "Mom, I'm an alcoholic, I'm gay, and I need help." (I figured I would tell her that I was both an alcoholic and gay at the same time so she would only need to feel half as bad about either circumstance.)

Mother found help. I entered the psychiatric hospital in my hometown where the director was a highly closeted gay man whom I knew. During this hospital stay I was introduced to Alcoholics Anonymous. A.A. in my hometown in 1979 was still pretty "redneck." I remember that at my first meeting a rather burly pipe fitter said to me, "Son, if you want to stay sober, you have to be honest." That immediately told me that "straight" A.A. was not for me.

Fortunately, about a week later, a counselor in the hospital asked me if I had ever heard of gay A.A. Wallowing in my feelings of being terminally unique, I replied, "Of course not." I was utterly flabbergasted. There went my million-selling novel. Someone else was just like me.

The counselor went on to tell me that the Detroit group, the only gay A.A. group in Michigan in 1979, met not far from my house. Amazing! I had lived in Detroit's "gay ghetto" throughout my drinking career, but I had never been aware of the extent of activities that comprised gay life until I sobered up.

I attended my first gay A.A. meeting with the assistance of an individual who later became my sponsor. I was mortified. It was the first time I would be around sober gay people. But the first meeting impressed me by the easy going banter of the members, the friendly humor, the loving energy, the attention I received, and the fact that this group of people knew how to have fun sober. We went out for ice cream after the meeting.

In a few weeks I felt as if I had always belonged to this group. The group met every other day, but I had to go two long days between Tuesday and Friday without a meeting. I remember how tough and long those two days used to be. It was this group and my sponsor that saved my life. They loved me when I could not love myself.

A couple of months later, I discovered the Higher Power. After a few more months of sobriety, I felt ready to do the 9th Step (making amends) with Bob. We had begun to see each other on a casual basis. I wanted a more intimate relationship with him, but he wouldn't have it until I was sober for a year. I was so mad I went out and found me a power higher than A.A., another "lover to take care of me." The guy I found didn't like my going to A.A.; it made him jealous. So I didn't go. After five months of using this guy (my conscience didn't improve with my just being dry), Bob decided it was time to "come out." As soon as he did, I broke up with the used-lover and went back to Bob. Bob wanted me to go back to A.A. I did go but, at first, to please him. Little did I know that this return to A.A. would start a wonderful "journey into happy destiny" which has taken me from Detroit, to Iowa, and on to Chicago, where I live today with Bob.

In the past nine years, I've discovered the benefits of "leading an examined life." I've felt the joy of unconditionally doing service for others, and I've experienced the harmony of making amends with others. "The promises" are ringing true in my life to the proportion by which I live a spiritual life. I'm becoming happily and usefully whole.

I've also practiced the 12 Steps in other areas besides

alcoholism. I quit smoking two years ago. I also dealt with problems of excessive lust a few years ago. And I've used the 12 Steps to work on my own homophobia so that I could accept being gay as a positive force in my life.

To do the latter task, I meditated on how being gay has benefited my life or the lives of others. This helped me see that perhaps God made me this way for a purpose. Next, I inventoried my fears, resentments, self pity, and relationship problems associated with being gay. This included people, institutions, and principles. I admitted those defects to another person and to God. I began to see where my fears about being gay affected my ability to be of service to other people. Next, I made amends to people with whom I had distorted relationships because I was not out to them. Today, my purpose for coming out to people is to increase the chance to harmonize our relationships. I generally tell people I'm gay, unless to do so would cause serious harm, such as getting fired. I do this so that my relationships with them can expand beyond the superficial. I try to be the same person all the time to everyone. This attitude has brought me great peace.

I am very active in gay A.A. service work. I have started, or have helped start, numerous gay A.A. meetings in rural areas, and I've co-founded a service group whose purpose is to provide outreach and education in the gay and lesbian communities concerning alcoholism. I continually learn more about alcoholism and how it affects us as gays and lesbians. These insights I share through writing, speaking at meetings, lecturing, researching, sponsoring, conducting workshops and seminars, and serving on various round-up and service group committees.

But I frequently forget a basic tenet of A.A. in all this activity: "Knowledge is not enough." I need, daily, to pray, to meditate, to read inspirational literature, and to talk to my A.A. friends. I also need to go to meetings, both gay and non-gay. I particularly enjoy the Twelve Step/Twelve Traditions and Big Book meetings. Most importantly, I try to be of service to others in my life, and I try to understand "what is the most loving thing I can do at any given moment."

Love is a very elusive thing. It is probably the one aspect of life I am learning the most about today, and need most to learn about. Sometimes love is gentle, sometimes it's confrontational. Sometimes I need to engage in activities of self-love, and sometimes I need to engage in selflessness. Many times I have to stop to listen to the voice in my heart, the voice that was not there when I drank. This is my conscience and intuition. It has developed considerably in sobriety and has become a working part of my mind.

I check my decisions if they involve major issues in my life or if they involve major decisions with others in A.A. I must remain a skeptic of my thoughts and feelings, as they can lead me into trouble if unreasoned. For a little part of me still wants to drink, and negative thoughts and emotions are the mechanisms by which I become ambushed. "The drink marks the end of the slip."

I also keep a journal of my life in sobriety. I have done so for five years now. This has enabled me objectively to review my life and the progress that I've made. The exercise of keeping a journal has enabled me to have faith when I'm in rough times, for I can see where the road has been rough before and how God brought me out of it. I can also see how activities I did several years ago influence events in my life today. This indicates that, perhaps, there is a divine guidance. This journal has also taught me that "now is not forever." If I just H.A.L.T. and wait, emotions will pass and I will be able more objectively to look at the reality in my life.

Finally, I am very excited about being part of gay A.A. and its recent tremendous growth worldwide. I especially like events such as "round-ups" and gay Alano clubs in our larger American cities. However, I hope in our enthusiasm we do not forget our rural gay and lesbian recovering alcoholic counterparts. I hope to see more correspondence between rural and urban gay/lesbian AA'ers. The A.A. message works well on the phone, in the mail, and on tape, and the message of gay sobriety can be especially important to those individuals who do not have much opportunity for positive gay or lesbian exposure. I mention this specifically because it has been shown to me over and over again that I must accept my being gay as a positive attribute in order to continue to grow spiritually, and to grow spiritually is my greatest insurance against relapse.

9

Flower Child

Almost two years ago, even though I was in a state of being as drunk as I had ever been, I experienced what is known as "moment of sanity." I was at the onset of yet another crisis for which I was directly responsible. In the past, I had gotten myself into many jams, but there was always someone there to bail me out. Each time, I had vowed to others and to myself that I was going to change. Then, as soon as the trouble passed, I would once again find myself in the same alcoholic behavior patterns. The only thing that had changed was that things were becoming progressively out of control. At an alarming rate, I was spiraling downward and becoming more deeply entrenched in the behaviors that I vowed to change when each time I was up against the wall.

I'll never forget that moment of sanity; nothing had ever seemed so clear. I knew that I could not allow myself to descend any lower. I could no longer put it off, for it was now or never, do or die. The truth was so obvious that I couldn't turn away from it. I had to do whatever it took to get clean and sober, although I had little faith that I could succeed. Looking back on the 35 years that went before that God-given moment, my story seems overwhelmingly long and windy. I can only attempt to keep it simple.

My years growing up were spent under unstable conditions. I began my life in the home of my grandparents. My mother had divorced my natural father before he knew that I was conceived. It was a very dysfunctional household in which I spent my first four years. My grandfather was an authoritarian and a perpetrator of much violence and chaos. Also at home were two uncles and an aunt, all of whom had definite psychological problems of their own. My mother worked much of the time to support us, so I became devoted to my grandmother. She was by far the least neurotic of the bunch.

The family was very ethnically Russian, my grandfather having come from the old country where heavy alcohol consumption was quite prevalent. I thought of excessive drinking as a very normal part of life. Whenever there was any kind of get together or celebration, heavy drinking was always involved. People would become very loud. They would laugh and sing loudly, and sometimes they would argue violently. This was reality to me; I knew no other way. Occasionally I was allowed to have a small glass of beer or wine or sips of a mixed drink. Despite the chaos and violence I observed, I was never personally abused, and I felt secure in that family. I was well cared for and loved.

When I was almost four years old, my mother married a man whom I keenly disliked. It was more than the typical stepfather/stepchild syndrome. He turned out to be a very detestable man, and we lived with him until I was seventeen. He was alcoholic, and he led my mother quite deliberately into alcoholism along with him for company and control. A clearly unctuous quality characterized the way he dealt with people outside and inside the home. And he possessed a tremendous need to dominate and control absolutely that intruded itself into all of his relations. In our relationship, his personality was played out in these ways. I was at all times expected to be perfect. It was imperative that I be unfailingly cheerful and charming, if I were just a little bit cranky on any given day, I was punished for it. If I got all A's on my report card except for one B, I was interrogated as to why that one B was not also an A. I was told how lazy I was. If a false charge was made against me by a neighbor and I tried to defend myself, I was called a liar. If I tried to speak up for myself about anything, I was insolent. My motives were always being examined, and the verdict was always negative. So, although I never suffered physical abuse, the mental abuse was devastating. I was programmed so consistently through the years to believe that I had all of these negative qualities lurking with me, that even though I loathed my stepfather and didn't value his opinions, his verbal assaults became my internal messages without my even being aware of it. My mother did the best she could to counteract his negative influence; I know that now. She gave me all the love she was capable of giving and many good examples to follow in the way of admirable qualities. I'm grateful to her for her efforts, but she was too much a victim of her own alcoholism and her belief in the helplessness of women to be effective in putting a stop to what was happening.

From my earliest memories onward, I was aware that I was attracted to members of my own sex, even when I was too young to know what sex was. I suppose I was more bisexual as a small child, and, then, given the male role models I had in my life, my homosexuality was just naturally cemented. I don't really look for any causes because it doesn't matter. I am gay, and I have no problems with being gay. I have never felt guilty about it. In my head, I have never felt that it was wrong, but it didn't take me long to realize how the rest of the world felt. I don't remember exactly what was said, but before I was even in school, I remarked something to my grandmother that concerned my feelings in ths area, and her reaction was so severely negative, that I knew that I was never to mention anything like that to anyone.

This was the beginning of a dangerous dichotomy in my thinking. I began to separate myself from the rest of the world. The world looked upon homosexuality as the most horrible thing in existence, and I didn't, I couldn't. So, there was the world in one corner and, in the other corner, was me. I was not included in the mainstream of humanity. My laws were different; I was an imposter who had to move cautiously in that other world.

My stepfather began working for the Federal Bureau of Prisons. Ours was a kind of military existence, in that we moved very frequently because he was transferred to different prisons. The first move was very traumatic because we moved to the other side of the country, three thousand miles away from the grandmother whom I loved so dearly and who represented the only security I had ever known. That was the beginning of my downward spiralling. It continued with our frequent relocations and my being the eternal new kid in school. That particular aspect of growing up never got any easier. As I grew, my sense of being different, especially because of my homosexual feelings, became more acute. With each new school that I walked into, I became increasingly insecure and shy. My sensitivity grew so raw that at times it engulfed me. And, of course, the advent of puberty made life even more difficult. I was intelligent, but not particularly masculine, so I immediately became a sexual suspect in every new situation I was thrust into. Adolescents can be ruthless to their peers when their peers don't conform to the stereotype behaviors of their gender. That kind of psychological climate was brutally conducive to tension and anxiety for me.

On the home-front, the tension and anxiety were also nearly intolerable. The alcoholism there, along with its attendant nightmares for me, was ever present. My mother and stepfather drank every day until they passed out. During my adolescence, every night ended in hair-raising screaming matches between my parents that sometimes erupted into physical violence. I would lie awake in bed at two o'clock in the morning, unable to sleep because outside my bedroom were hysterical and profane shouting, locked doors being pounded on, and telephones being ripped out of the wall. As I grew older, relationships between my stepfather and myself continued to grow less and less cordial, until they were openly hostile on both sides. The course of our lives through the years are too complicated for me to detail, but it culminated in my running away from home when I was seventeen years old, just after high school graduation. I was brought back and immediately sent East to live with my grandmother. Shortly thereafter, my mother finally plucked up the courage to leave my stepfather.

Although alcohol was never a stranger to me, I can certainly remember the first time I really drank and got drunk. It was like coming home. I felt relaxed and uninhibited; that was the greatest thing about it for me. When I drank, I could do anything I wanted, and all of the insecurities and feelings of inferiority were gone. I, who had always felt buried alive, was released with alcohol. I could jettison my self-imposed tethers and become the real me. Being about fifteen years old at the time, I quickly became aware of yet another bonus to the whole drinking deal. Not only did it liberate me, but it was an easy avenue to help gain acceptance from my peers. And to top it off, I was so good at it! They respected that sort of thing. I can remember consciously thinking that here, at last, was something I could do to gain approval, and so I was determined to be better at it than anyone else. Unfortunately, for me, that's what happened. After the first time I got drunk, there were periods of time in my life when I didn't drink very often, but I know that every time I did drink, I most certainly drank alcoholically.

My teens and early 20's were spent in "the Sixties," and I was quite an enthusiastic flower child. This was a time of great changes in social and moral customs, and there was a great excitement in the air. A fresh wind blew across the nation, and the feeling of liberation on all fronts was exhilarating. I found it all wonderful because all of the old rules were disregarded. Any heretofore unthinkable behaviors were liberally accepted (or so it seemed), and many of my generation were striving to be freaks. I, who had always felt like a freak, became less of a sore thumb. Not only was I able to blend in and become more camouflaged, I could even feel a little superior with the knowledge that I was the real thing, the genuine article. I didn't have to try or pretend to be offbeat. I had been right all along, and my time had come.

Unfortunately, with that era also came unrestrained drug experimentation. All clinical knowledge and common sense about recreational drug use were cavalierly dismissed as being not only unfounded, but ridiculous. We were very clever and knew everything. Drug use became another proof of my acceptability. I tried just about everything except heroin, and that was only because (by the grace of God) it was somehow the one drug whose path I never encountered. Had it ever been offered, I would've done it. When I first used methamphetamine, I knew, just as I had with alcohol, that it was something I had been waiting for all of my life. Today I know that, without a doubt, I was an alcoholic and speed freak long before I ever picked up either substance.

In my early twenties, I used any drug that I got my hands on. In addition, I drank alcohol with each of the other drugs I used. I developed a serious addiction to speed which I eventually started taking intravenously. At one point, after having been strung out and burnt out on speed for a lengthy period, I happened to swallow a very bad dose of LSD which left me to suffer for years with horrendous anxiety attacks. I was convinced that I was psychotic, and I became agoraphobic - afraid to leave my home. I had gone to several psychiatrists who gave me no answers but who provided me with the opportunity to become dependent on tranquilizers. I must have had every tranquilizer in the book prescribed to me at one time or another. At one point, my psychiatrist had me on five different tranquilizers at once. I was so heavily medicated, that my speech was slurred and I could not function very well. It was then decided that I should check into a psychiatric hospital for a few weeks. That turned out to be a complete waste of time. They really didn't offer me anything that I needed, so I came away feeling more lost and hopeless than when I had gone in.

Then, by sheer willpower, I somehow extricated myself from those addictions. I still drank a lot at times and occasionally smoked pot, but I stayed clear of speed and tranquilizers. I felt somewhat better, of course, but I still had no skills with which to deal with my emotional problems, so I still experienced a lot of problems with anxiety and depression. I was moving in no particular direction.

When I hit my mid-twenties, I finally met some other gay people and eagerly lunged headlong into the gay world. I thought that I was finally going home, that I would be with people just like me and that I would finally live in a world where I belonged. I had envisioned a loving, compassionate fraternity, but I was thoroughly disillusioned. I found that I felt even more like an alien in gay society than I did in the straight world. My internal message was that I really was, after all, a freak.

I felt intellectually and culturally foreign to the men I was seeing in bars. I was appalled by my observations of how these gay men were treating each other. I resented and felt threatened by the games I saw being played. I was shocked by the hostility that I saw which existed between gay men and lesbians. I couldn't understand much of anything that I was seeing, especially since it was all so contrary to the ideal that I had conceived of how it would be.

I thought that it was sad that basically the only place to congregate in the gay world was in a gay bar. Almost anyone could become an alcoholic under those circumstances, and I was very ready. I drank to become someone else - someone who could deal with it all, someone who could play the games, someone who didn't care. When I drank, I was less insecure and more outgoing. I was so truly witty that I was very entertaining and, I thought, brilliant. I fell into the "life of the party" role and always felt duty bound to give a good performance. I was the one who created the character that I had become, but later I began to resent my audience for expecting to see a show. Gradually, I became more and more disgusted with what I saw myself becoming, but I insisted on continuing to play at being the party clown. I didn't know what else to do.

Another important aspect of my drinking was the liberating effect it had on me sexually. When I was drunk, I could be sexually uninhibited and promiscuous. In fact, I could only be that way when I was drinking, and so I really began drinking a lot. It never dawned on me just to accept my natural inclination to be discriminating. I also suffered from a major "Cinderella complex," and I thought that this situation would only be temporary because, certainly, Prince Charming would one day appear and take me away to live with him happily ever after. To increase my chances of finding this savior, I thought it only logical to go out into the field as often as possible, and I set to my task with an unflappable dedication. For a time it was fun. But time kept moving on with no prospects in sight, and it started to become more difficult to make bed-hopping fun. I had to increase my alcohol consumption to keep myself in the right frame of mind so as not to stray from my goal. I was out in the bars every night drinking wildly and waking up with terrible hangovers and with men whose names I could not recall. Then, I would have to spend a great deal of time in unfamiliar neighborhoods trying to locate where in the world I had parked my car. Throughout all this, I was becoming progressively less responsible with financial matters.

I can vaguely recall that period of time when things first began subtly to get out of control. I was arrested in a blackout for drunk driving when I ran into a parked car. I eventually got out of that charge through sheer luck. Shortly thereafter, I was in another accident for which I was not arrested. I was, however, so disgusted with myself that I attempted suicide. Fortunately, that attempt was thwarted by the intervention of friends, and I was forced to vomit for about half an hour in a hospital emergency room.

I was miserable and felt lost. I began therapy again so that I could find the answers that would make everything miraculously fall into place. I had convinced myself that I must be crazy and that there was some elusive psychological key that was causing all of my problems. I knew by now that I was an alcoholic, but I didn't believe alcoholism was what was making me miserable. I did go to an A.A. meeting, but decided it wasn't for me. It didn't seem like being an alcoholic was so bad. I wasn't like some of the other people I saw who had drinking problems. No matter how much I drank, I always spoke coherently, could always walk without stumbling, and could usually retain most of my memory. I would become disgusted when I saw people who were so drunk that they couldn't handle themselves. It didn't occur to me that even though I probably drank more than some of these people, it was only my outward skills that were somehow less affected, but that my life was becoming just as unmanageable as the drunk who couldn't stand up. My denial in alcoholism came in the area of progression. I thought that I would always be able to maintain a certain level of frequency of drinking in my alcoholism, that I could control it. When my disease did begin to progress, I strove not to stop drinking but to return to a more functional and acceptable level of alcoholism.

In addition to alcohol, other drugs came into the picture again and showed me that the progression of hard drug abuse could begin and accelerate with a swiftness that was beyond my ability to control. After I had ended my first addiction to hard drugs by my own willpower, I stayed away from them completely for several years. Then I began to snort speed and to take diet pills occasionally for the next couple of years. Eventually, as the forces within me began to become more turbulent, I one day decided to try taking the speed by injection again. Within a couple of months, I was at a place that I hadn't previously known existed. It became my new home. I found myself with people and in situations and involved in habits of living that I had thought were below my possibilities of reaching. The people I lived with told me I had to stop or get out, but I did want to stop. There were several times, when I was really strung out, that I stood in front of a mirror and gouged at my face with my fingernails because I felt so ugly inside, and there was another suicide attempt. I thought I could stop drug abuse on my own just as I had done before, but I found that, despite how much I wanted to, I couldn't.

In trying to abstain from drugs other than alcohol, my alcohol intake increased by leaps and bounds. And, of course, when I was drunk I would want to shoot some dope and lacked the willpower to say no to myself. Eventually, I was caught and asked to leave by my roommates. It was ironic because they were both in the throes of alcohol addiction at the time, but my drug addiction was so horrendous that it made their problems seem mild by comparison. They are both in recovery now.

I got this horrible little room by myself and continued in my addictions for about another year and a half. I was curbing the drug use pretty well, but I always got around to having another slip. The progression of my alcoholism just thrived. I drank around the clock, beginning from the moment I woke up. I would finish the rest of the drink by my bed that was left over from when I had passed out the night before, even before I got up to go to the bathroom. I had always had a drink with me wherever I went, and when I went to work I had liquor in my car and could go out on my breaks and down a few. By this time, I had to drink at least every couple of hours or else I would begin to get dry heaves and to feel as if my mind was coming unhinged. Towards the end of this period of my life, I was on the verge of losing my job.

Emotionally, I was in an abyss. Everything was dark and frightening. Every aspect of my life was falling apart and becoming worse on a daily basis. The more I drank, the more frightened I became; and the more frightened I became, the more I drank to dispel my fears. I clung desperately to the delusion that things weren't as bad as they seemed and that I could somehow be able to return to my former, more manageable level of alcoholism. If I could get back to that level, I wouldn't have to give up alcohol completely, and giving up alcohol completely was a thought that I simply could not bear to consider. Physically, I was quite done in. I felt very sick all of the time. I couldn't keep food down and was also beginning to have trouble controlling my bowels. Yet, I refused to let myself see that things were already careening so far out of control that an end of one sort or another had to come.

I was very lucky. That end came before I lost everything, and it came with that moment of sanity. I knew that I couldn't ask anyone to help me anymore until I did something to help myself, and that "something" was surrendering to the fact that I could not drink or use drugs at all ever again. I had fought so hard and for so long to hold out, but I was finally at the bottom with nowhere further down to go.

A very dear friend came over and made the arrangements for me to enter a detox unit. After the arrangements were made, he called my job to tell them I wouldn't be able to come to work for a while and why. This call was made five minutes after I was supposed to have started working, and I knew that I might get fired, but it didn't matter anymore. All of my excuses were exhausted and invalid. The only thing that mattered anymore was that I begin to get help for my problem, and that I begin immediately. In that moment, I was faced with making a decision whether I wanted to live or to die. It was that simple, and I chose to live.

I was in the detox unit for five days. The first day, I had to stay in bed because I almost had a seizure from withdrawal. I wound up having to take an anticonvulsant for three days. The next four days were the most structured days that I had lived in years. I went to workshops, individual therapy, group therapy, and various self-help group meetings such as A.A. and N.A. I was given a physical exam and had blood work done and was told that, physically, this was my last chance for recovery. The staff was comprised mostly of recovering alcoholic people who had a lot to offer me. This had a lot to do with disposing me to be ready and willing to take what they had to offer; I wanted it. It was the same with meetings. I was ready to listen, and so I heard what I needed to hear. I received the first reward of A.A., and that is hope.

I was frightened when I came out of the hospital and had very little faith in myself that I would actually be able to maintain sobriety. I had never succeeded at anything before, for I had never been able to stick with anything long enough to succeed at it. But I took the hope that I had been given in those meetings and went out into the world determined to give it my best try and to do whatever it took to remain free from alcohol and other mind-altering drugs.

I immediately called an addictions therapist who had been recommended by the hospital and began working with him. I got myself to A.A. meetings. I kept going back to meetings and listening to what was being said. I found out that I wasn't alone and that many other people had experienced the same horrors that I had. I learned the things that they did to aid in their recovery. I had a desire to stop drinking and an openness and willingness to change.

Two important words in my recovery have been "change" and "choices." It has been such a remarkable concept for me to realize that I do have choices in my life and that I can choose to change those things that are unacceptable to me, if only I believe I possess the courage to change. To empower myself, I never forget the Serenity Prayer. That prayer has been a very powerful tool for me; it has clarified for me just what those things are over which I do and do not have control.

I couldn't be more grateful to the fellowship of A.A. Two years ago I felt broken and beyond repair. I thought that A.A. would turn out to be something that worked for other people but not for me. But I found out that the tools of the program would work for me if I was willing to use them, and that I, too, had the capacity to mature and grow and to be able to practice the A.A. principles in all of my affairs. I thought that, in embracing A.A., I would have to lose myself when, instead, I began to find myself. I was threatened by the concept of a higher power and thought that God was just a crutch for the weak. Then I began to experience the joys of spirituality and have learned that God is a foundation of strength.

Abstinence from alcohol and other drugs was only the beginning. It is from continued growth that we reach true sobriety, and it is by continuing to go to meetings and by following through on the desire to learn about the tools of A.A. that we can achieve that growth. But it's not always easy. This second year has been in some ways harder than the first, not harder in terms of abstinence, but in terms of maintaining emotional stability. After the pink cloud of the first year wore off a bit, I found that I really had to start facing some issues and working through them, for they had contributed to my disease. When things got a little overwhelming, I just clung on to the hope I had been given at that first meeting, and I kept coming back and entrusting more faith in that higher power that has carried me such a long way already. I picked up the tools of the program and kept moving forward, and things started getting better. I feel that I'm really getting sober now, and I see that my life can just keep opening up wider and higher as long as I don't get in my own way.

That's the best thing about A.A. If you use its tools when you need them, A.A. works. Anyone can feel good about A.A. when feeling good and things are going well. But it's during the tough times that one really has the opportunity to put A.A. to use and to watch it work. My life is so different from what it was two years ago that I wonder how I possibly could've lived it. But I know that if I pick up a drink or use other drugs, I'll be right back there or dead. Therefore, I have to stay sober one day at a time through the program of Alcoholics Anonymous. Today I have health, self-respect, self-love, wonderful friends, and a future that promises that I can realize my full potential as a human being if I am willing to work at it. And for these things, I am truly grateful.

10

Go with the Flow

My name is John. I grew up in a farming town on the prairies of South Dakota. My first recollections of how I related to the rest of the world were that I didn't fit in. I realized, when I was about thirteen, that I was very attracted to men. I remember the time when I first realized that I was homosexual. I don't remember how I figured it out, but I knew that I had a secret that no one must ever know about. I was also sure that I had to be the only homosexual in the world or certainly in South Dakota. From that time on, I set out to cover up who I really was.

My world told me I was a sissy. All of the guys I grew up with, who were mostly sons of farmers, talked of sports, cars, and crops - of a million things that I could have cared less about. I knew people were talking about me behind my back, so at a very early age I developed defense mechanisms to deal with them. Through my defense mechanisms, I moved more and more into myself, until finally my whole world existed in my head. I wanted very much to fit in somewhere, to have a friend, and to be able to tell him, or her, who I really was and how much I really hurt. My parents were very loving, very conservative, and very strict. I never doubted that they loved me and that I loved them, but I certainly couldn't tell them who I was. I was very lonely.

I went to college in another South Dakota town in the '60's. It was the Vietnam war era, and I was about to be drafted, so I enlisted in the Navy and spent four years on active duty. All this time I still maintained my cover about my homosexuality. I had a top secret security clearance in the Navy, which would never have been issued to a suspected homosexual. I was covering up all the way. During my Navy days, I began to drink, nearly always on weekend bashes and usually by myself.

I had dated girls throughout high school, and I had a

girlfriend a good part of the time I was in the Navy and in college. I dated several girls after college and decided that I would probably never get married. Then I met a girl who was really on fire to get married, and I decided that, if I were ever going to get married, I might as well marry this woman. So, at age twenty-five, I got married. We had our first child when I was twenty-six; and our second when I was thirty.

My wife and I were very involved in our church (one of the holy roller, full-gospel denominations). Our lives centered around the church and church work. I tried very hard to fit in. Even as an adult, always covering up who and what I really was, I never found a place where I was completely comfortable, or a person with whom I was truly at ease.

Of course, being so involved in the church, I did very little drinking. As the years passed, however, slowly I started to have a few drinks just because I was so uncomfortable with the life I was living. On the outside, I seemed to have it all - a white house with green shutters in the suburbs, a loving wife, two happy kids, two cars, and even a friendly family dog. I and my family were the picture of the perfect middle-class family. I had everything that typified a perfectly contented life. But on the inside, I was miserable. I loved my kids and my wife, but the life I had with them was a fraud. I was simply acting in nearly all areas of my life - pretending that my life was fulfilling, and deceiving everyone by behaving as if my church and God were the center of my life. The truth was that much of my behavior was faked, most of my life was a sham, and I was basically an imposter.

I had never had a gay sexual experience in my life. I had bought some books and done some reading, but had never experienced anything personally. I longed to live as the person that I really was. Of course, all this filled me with guilt - guilt which I kept completely to myself. Had I told anyone about the guilt I was feeling, I would have had to explain why, and I certainly wasn't going to do that. Finally, our marriage began to suffer. My wife had some emotional insecurities that contributed to our marital problems. But, for me, the problem was mostly the lack of fulfillment in the life I was living. We sought help in the church and began marriage counseling on a weekly basis. I began to drink again. I would drink only once in a while, and it would bring so much relief to me. Drinking was the great escape from all the pain and frustration.

I had also done a lot of praying that God would heal me of my homosexuality and let me be happy in my marriage. I sought the Lord for help in all the things that I did every day but those things meant so little to me. No answers ever came; no peace ever descended. I started gradually drinking a little more.

Years before our marital problems started, my wife and I had begun to work closely with another couple in the church in a children's ministry. After working together for several years, we became close friends and did things together socially. Ned, the husband, and I found that we had some common interests and enjoyed spending time together and working on projects together. After we had been friends for eight years or so, one weekend I, my wife and our kids, and Ned, his wife and his kids went to visit my in-laws. I was drinking regularly by this time, so I got some wine, and Ned and I started drinking. I got pretty drunk and told him that I was gay. He confessed to me that he was also gay, and we began an affair.

I had experienced some guilt in the past, but nothing like the guilt I experienced after having some homosexual experiences. I knew that fulfillment lay in being able to be gay and to relax with it, but from where I sat, there was no way I could ever attain that state of mind. I felt guilty because I knew that God would never approve of what I was doing, that the church would never approve, and that my wife and children didn't deserve this infidelity. But I now had proof that I was homosexual, though I was convinced that I would never be able to live as one.

My drinking increased rapidly during and after the affair with Ned. I finally confessed in the marriage counseling that I had a problem with homosexuality, and that began several years of personal counseling on my sexuality. Our church counselors were going to heal me of this terrible sin. My wife and I would go for one session each week for marriage counseling, and I would go for one session for counseling on my sexuality.

I had a lifetime of pain to try to deal with. Christian counseling deals with what you should do in light of God's teaching in the Bible. Well, there was nothing about John that the Bible approved of. After several years of counseling, every aspect of my life, my thinking, my interests, my goals - everything - had been gone over. None of it was acceptable in God's eyes, and it all had to be changed. I was convinced that everything about me was bad or unacceptable.

My wife had come from a very conservative Midwestern upbringing and was totally homophobic. She absolutely could not deal with the fact that I was gay. For several years we tried to work through some of the problems, but only got further and further from each other. I cannot blame her for being unable to deal well with our situation; she was just incapable of doing it.

During the years of counseling, I was drinking almost on a daily basis. Our home was about thirty miles from where I worked. I would ride in a car-pool which would let me off at a shopping center where I left my car. I would go into the drugstore or liquor store and buy what I was going to drink for the night. I would drink half a bottle of wine or take several swigs from a bottle of vodka so that I had a buzz when I got home. During the course of the evening, I would drink perhaps two more bottles of wine, or one half to three quarters of a bottle of vodka.

My wife had never been around an alcoholic before, so she didn't realize how much I was drinking. Every night when I'd get home from work, I would sit with her and have a glass of wine or perhaps a drink. This was my strategy to explain the smell of liquor on my breath that would persist throughout the night. Then, every half hour or so, I would go to the place where I had hidden my bottle and just tip it up. As the evening wore on, I got drunker and drunker.

I felt that I was a good father, despite my troubled life and marriage. I really loved my children, but I was in so much emotional pain that I don't know what quality of relationship we had. I really did try to be everything a good father should be to his children. But being gay, I believed, I would always fall short. Of course, I didn't realize that it was the drinking that was removing me emotionally from them.

I remember telling myself once during this time that life is bad, it will always be bad, and I will have to live this way the rest of my life. I now realize that I unconsciously also added to that creed that I was going to keep myself in a drunken stupor, so that I wouldn't have to feel so much of the pain.

My only escape was alcohol. I drank every day - always in the evening when I got home. I usually went to sleep in a stupor or just passed out. As the years passed, my wife still had no idea of the large amount of alcohol I was consuming each day. I never missed a day of work because of drinking, and I always got the things done that I had to do. I was extremely conscientious toward fulfilling my obligations, and I would do all I could to complete them; then I would get drunk. I never thought about doing anything any differently. My life was completely automatic. I would do the yard work on the weekend - in the heat for hours and hours. As soon as it was done, I got drunk.

My drinking, too, was done thoughtlessly. I even began drinking when we entertained people from the church, and I would have a few drinks before going to the counseling sessions. My drinking developed to the point that I just always drank. It never occurred to me that it was a problem. I don't even recall ever consciously telling myself that if I drank, then it would dull some of the miserable life I was existing through. My drinking began unconsciously, and that's the way it continued.

One day, finally, my wife said that she didn't think she could go on trying to deal with my homosexual problem any longer. She felt that we should have a trial separation.

We had stayed together for the sake of our children, but were beginning to realize the harm we were doing to them. Our home was filled with tension all the time. No one ever talked about the problems in front of the kids, but they knew things were not right. We agreed that I would move out in the summer and let the kids have the summer to adjust. When school was out, I sat down with my children and told them the situation. I took them to see my new apartment and told them that they could visit me and that we would spend time together. After I moved to my own little apartment, I was still trying to live as a straight man; I couldn't confront my homosexuality. I joined organizations for divorced parents - a wonderful opportunity to go out and drink. I was trying to be there for my children, whom I now saw only on weekends. Every night I would go to my little apartment and get drunk. And I cried...I cried for a friend; I cried for the relationship that I wanted with my kids; I cried because life seemed to be nothing but worthless desperation. I felt very alone and very trapped - trapped in a world that I didn't know how to get out of. The only escape was to drink.

One day I decided that it was time that I take some control of my life. I decided that the only way to do that was to try to figure out who I really was. Of course, that involved finding out about this homosexuality matter that I had never dealt with, except to bury it or escape from it in alcohol. Through all the counseling in the church, I had come to feel that I was not entitled to feel good about just being the person that I was, so I had tried to change everything. Somehow, through all the alcohol and all the pain, I knew that there was a worthwhile person somewhere inside. I had been taught that I was a bad person, but I was beginning to think otherwise. What the church counselor had said just didn't make sense.

I decided that I had to take some steps to find out where I belonged and who I was. I decided that taking a step was all that I could do. So, ten months after moving out of the house, I moved into the center of the city, into the heart of the gay community. I knew I didn't know what I was doing, but I had to do something. Even a step that turns out to be the wrong one is better than no step at all when you are where I was.

I found a little apartment which I could not afford, set up housekeeping and started poking my nose into the gay lifestyle. I had become such a regular drinker by this point, that it was nothing to get up enough courage to enter the gay bars after eight or ten shots of whiskey at the apartment. Drunk, I had the courage I needed to step out.

I worked endless overtime to pay the apartment rent, the excessive child support I was paying out of guilt, and to support my drinking. I would go to work in the morning with a terrible hangover, work until 8:30 or 9:00 at night, go home and get drunk and go to the bars. But I couldn't make meaningful contact anywhere. I did manage to make a few drinking buddies, but I was looking for sincerity and fulfillment, for something to take hold of and make a life with. I was looking for a permanent love relationship with another man. Not finding this, I continued to feel empty.

It still had not occurred to me during this time that my drinking was a problem. It never had. I never tried to slow down my drinking or to stop. It never occurred to me that perhaps walking in the door at night and having four shots of whiskey before I even took my coat off was unusual, though that was exactly my behavior. Immediately when I would get home, a terrible, desperate loneliness would sweep over me. A few shots would always make it go away. I also experienced plenty of bad hangovers, but I kept telling myself that I needed to try to figure out some way not to feel so sick in the morning. Never did I consider that I should stop drinking.

Then the blackouts started. I would wake up in the morning and have whole blocks of time from the night before that were missing. I would spend time with my kids and not remember part of it. I could remember taking them in the car, but not bringing them back home. Only when the blackouts began recurring did I begin to think that maybe I needed to do some serious thinking about how much I was drinking. I was beginning to involve other people in my irresponsible actions, and I was endangering other people's lives. This awareness finally prompted me to action.

I went to my first A.A. meeting over two years ago. It was a gay traditions meeting. I didn't understand much of what was going on, but that was okay. I met a friendly man named Jim, who said he was going to another meeting after that one, and he invited me to go along. It was another gay A.A. meeting. After that second meeting, I knew that there was something here that might help me get my drinking straightened out. People seemed to take an interest in me, which, in itself, made me more interested in gay A.A., as I was so desperate for friendship.

After that second meeting, I knew I was qualified to be in A.A. I liked the gay A.A. meetings because I realized that the issues they dealt with were the ones that I needed to deal with, too. Here I could deal with the drinking and with being gay. And I could meet gay people who were not sitting in a bar with long faces, afraid to say "Hello" like I was.

For the first few weeks, I just went to a meeting every night. I didn't realize, when I started regularly going to the meetings, that it would mean that I would have a place to go every night, something to do every night. I had no problem going to ninety meetings in ninety days because, without the drinking, there was nothing else to do anyway.

I got a sponsor after a couple of weeks. We became good friends and spent many hours talking on the phone. Because of my experiences in the church, I had a real problem with all the God talk in the meetings. I had a bitter resentment against God and anything related to Him. My sponsor told me that I shouldn't worry about that for now. He told me just to go to meetings and not to drink. He said that I would have a lot of time to get the God stuff figured out later on. I followed his advice and just went to meetings.

Slowly, I started to make friends in the program. I

started to have things to do in my life besides work and drink and feel bad. I felt that I had been through a great deal, and that I had a lot of pain in my life, but I learned that there are a lot of people who say the same thing. Most importantly, I learned that you can pick yourself up from where you are and go on.

I began to get the idea that life isn't going to be perfect, that I'm not going to be perfect, that my relationships with other people aren't going to be perfect, because this isn't a perfect world. I began to get the idea that in the midst of all this imperfection I could still have a fulfilled life. I began to learn to "go with the flow."

There were a lot of days when I still hurt bad. But I began to try living "one day at a time," instead of looking at the future and all the potential for pain that it holds, and life started to get better. It started to have a little meaning. And, most of all, I began to realize that the person that I am is okay, that what I needed to do was just to find out who I was. I don't have to be perfect; I just have to try to live each day as well as I can. Every day doesn't have to be spectacular; it just needs to be lived. All those things that I was trying to hide from the world, I can let them out - can let them out and find out who I am. I have a disease, but I need to remember that I now am in recovery.

I remember that, one day after a lunch meeting, I was on my way back to the office when, suddenly, I was so filled with gratitude because I actually felt like an "ordinary" person. I had never felt like an ordinary person in my entire life. I had spent thirty-eight years feeling like a totally worthless person.

When I walked into that first gay A.A. meeting, I had a vague idea that maybe I would figure out how not to drink so much. I had no idea that in A.A. I would find a whole meaning to life. Now, two years after that first meeting, I know I am a worthwhile person. I haven't accomplished much of what I hope to in my life, but I know now that I have the potential to accomplish anything that I want. Even more important than that, I know that because of A.A., no matter what I do accomplish or don't, I will be okay. I still have problems with my ex-wife and have a very strained relationship with my children, but I do what I can and then turn it over. I have friends for the first time in my life - real friends. They make me feel that they enjoy being with me, as much as I enjoy being with them. I don't have a lover, but I have dated some people who've become very special to me. I know one day that I will have a lover, and I want to experience that before I die, but it doesn't have to happen tomorrow or next year. When H.P. (Higher Power) decides it's right, then it will be the time.

One of the big issues during the first year was God. I started referring to my Higher Power as H.P. There were spiritual things happening to me, but I didn't know where they came from. Because of my past experiences with God, I just couldn't believe that the Christian God actually cared about me. My sponsor said that sometimes people make A.A. itself their Higher Power. That made no sense when he said it, but I kept it in mind.

Today, A.A. is my Higher Power. During all those years in the church, I was looking for an assurance that I was loved. I have found that in A.A. I was looking for somewhere to take my problems where there was an answer. I have found that in A.A.. A.A. doesn't always solve all the problems in my life, but it certainly gives me a healthy way to deal with them. A.A. is always there, ready and waiting to see me through anything that life throws at me - a place to share the good stuff and a place to share the bad stuff. Maybe someday the Christian God and I will be friends, but, for now, A.A. is my Higher Power.

I don't get to a meeting every day any more. I actually have other things going on in my life now. But I do make sure that I get to at least four meetings a week, and I try to make five or six. My life began in A.A., and I know that in order to continue this life, I still need lots of contact with it. I don't go to meetings because I feel that I should, or because I have to, or because my sponsor tells me to. I go to meetings because I like to. It is the part of my life that keeps me together, happy and calm. It is the whole meaning to my life right now.

As for the lover issue - for a long time I felt that if I had a lover, my life would have some special meaning, and I would be a very happy person. Through the program, I have learned that you cannot let another person be for you the entire meaning of your existence or the only source of your happiness. My life is happy these days. I still hope to have that lover one day, but he will not give me my meaning for life or my happiness. He will be a very nice addition to my already happy life. With this in mind, I know that I will choose the right person, and, if he chooses me, I now feel that I am worthy of being chosen.

Thank you, A.A., for giving me my life.

11

Happiness Is an Inside Job

My name is Ted. I live in Oklahoma City and this is my story. Most of my life I have sought escapes because I was unwilling to accept the reality of the life I was living. I fantasized about the future, regretted the past and paid little attention to the present. I can't remember being happy with myself, until I finally found a better way to live through the program of Alcoholics Anonymous. I spent a lot of time looking for happiness through people, places and things, but today I know my happiness is an inside job; it is not contingent upon outside sources.

I was an unhappy, miserable child. I didn't like myself or my family. I often wished I'd been born to a different family; I didn't feel loved by them, nor did I feel that I loved them. I couldn't wait to be an adult.

I fell in love for the first time in my life when I was sixteen years old. I was living in Great Falls, Montana, and I'd made a new friend; his name was Kirk. He was very athletic, handsome and fun to be with, and I couldn't believe he actually liked me and enjoyed spending time with me. I didn't admit my love for Kirk to myself or to anyone else, least of all to Kirk. Deep inside I knew I was gay, but I didn't tell anyone, and I was determined to fight the gay feelings and suppress them.

I was very confused about love, not knowing what it meant to love someone or to be loved. I tried to please Kirk in every way so that he would continue to love me. This started an unhealthy pattern of dependency and manipulating that would be a part of my personality for many years. I had a terrible fear that if I didn't do exactly as a friend expected, I would lose him. This fear grew more with each person I loved and interfered with all my relationships.

Eventually I moved to Salt Lake City, Utah. There I made a new friend, Terry, who was like Kirk in many ways. Terry became my closest friend, and I began to fall in love with him, but I wouldn't do anything to show or express how I felt. People at work noticed that we were together often, and one day someone asked Terry if he were gay. He said he wasn't, but asked this co-worker why he wanted to know. The response was, "I see you with your friend all the time, so I just assumed you were gay, too." A bystander who had heard the conversation told me what had been said, and I was very upset. Terry tried to tell me that it didn't matter, but I was convinced that anyone who was my friend was automatically suspected also of being gay. This made me angry. I didn't admit I was gay. I denied my homosexual feelings and was fighting all urges very strongly. I didn't want to be gay. Terry suspected what I was doing in my head and wisely urged me to seek psychiatric help, which I did.

The psychiatric therapy helped, but it was a slow process and the situation at work seemed to get worse. I was working on changing my behavior so that people would not assume I was gay, but their assumptions remained. I went into a very deep depression. Thinking that I would never change and wanting to die, I took an overdose of pills. The number of pills I took weren't enough to kill me, and so I began the painful ordeal of recovering after the attempt at suicide.

In time I decided I wanted to enjoy life, and I began to socialize with people again. I was invited to a party where I knew alcohol would be served, and I accepted the invitation. Prior to this party, I had only tasted beer and wine; I wanted to know what it was like to have a real drink. My curiosity was strong. I drank, got drunk and loved it. Physically, I got sick, but before getting sick I had the fantastic psychological experience that drunkenness often brings. I had so much fun at that party, I talked a lot, and people seemed to like me. I didn't feel like the depressed little fag I always thought myself to be; I felt great. I liked myself when I was drunk, and I felt others liked me, too. My problems seemed to disappear, and I realized that being drunk was the greatest escape I had ever had. I knew that I would try drinking to get drunk again.

Soon I became concerned because I began to get drunk more often than I had expected, and I certainly didn't want to turn into an alcoholic. So I made some drinking rules. I decided that I would never drink alone and that I would never drink prior to going to work or while I was on the job. I followed my rules, but continued to drink.

After a period of more moving, I eventually returned to my childhood home state of Michigan and enrolled at Oakland University in suburban Detroit. My first roommate in the dorm that year was a great looking guy named Paul. He was a few months younger than I, tall, dark, handsome, and very athletic — just my type, and I knew it the minute I saw him. I also knew he wasn't gay, but that didn't stop me from fantasizing. Paul and I became close friends, but I never told him my secret feelings about him.

The first time Paul and I got drunk together, we stayed in our room and closed the door because we didn't want anyone else to know what we were doing. No one on campus had ever seen Paul or me drink. We both had reputations as "good" boys, and we weren't sure we wanted to ruin those reputations in one night. Actually, I was only in one of my many "no drinking" periods, which I forced myself into whenever I felt guilty for drinking too much too often. After that night we decided we didn't care about our reputations and began to surprise people by showing up at parties and drinking.

Paul left Oakland, and I met Doug. In retrospect it seems my life changed overnight when I met him; everything happened so fast. I fell in love immediately, and before I realized what was happening, I was in one of the sickest relationships of my life. Doug was fantastic; he was handsome, fun to be with, very popular, and I adored him. In the beginning he spent long hours talking with me, trying to help with my many problems. We shared secrets with each other, including some sexual secrets. Doug lost his virginity while we were friends. When he needed someone to talk to about it, he chose me. I told him how I had felt when I had had sex with a woman for the first time, but I never told him that I loved him and that I wanted to have sex with him.

Unlucky me....Doug was not gay, and our relationship was never sexual, but that was only because he had never asked or indicated he wanted anything sexual from me. I certainly wanted him, but I chose to suppress my desires. I did anything to keep him near me. I tried to supply his every need, and, most of the time, his needs came before mine. I did his laundry, cleaned his room, typed his homework papers, did anything to make Doug realize he needed me. The biggest fear in my life was that Doug wouldn't like me anymore.

Doug and I went to Salt Lake City in the summer of 1981. If I could go back in time and erase that entire summer, I would. Doug and I spent a lot of time together, entirely too much time. Finally, he began to see how dependent I had become on him, and he felt trapped. I was extremely depressed and talked of suicide often. I walked to work and cried all the way, hiding my face from people passing by. I arrived at work and ran into the bathroom to wash my face before any of the other employees saw me. This was almost a daily routine. I felt trapped in my depression and could not see a way out.

Doug was working two jobs but eventually quit his night job, because he was afraid to leave me home alone. We got into an argument one night. During it, he let me know that he was sick of the suicide talk and that he couldn't help me anymore. He told me either to get professional help or that he was going to call my mother to arrange to get help for me. I didn't want my mother involved in this situation, so I agreed to get the professional help.

The therapist I began to see was understanding about my feelings for Doug and let me talk about him at every session. He knew I was in love with Doug, and he encouraged me to explore my feelings about being gay. We worked on breaking my unhealthy dependence on Doug and on accepting the fact that I was gay, but I wasn't ready for the help this therapist was offering.

In late July, Doug hurt me badly. I thought I would never speak to him again. He announced he was going back to Michigan with or without me. He knew I didn't have enough money to leave Utah, and I knew that this was his way of telling me that he had to get away. I felt he was abandoning me. I felt apart emotionally, and I was very angry with him. I called my therapist, who asked me to come in to see him. While in his office, he asked me to check myself into the psychiatric unit of a hospital for suicidal depression. He was afraid that when Doug left, I would try to kill myself. But I wanted to stay with Doug for as long as he was still in Utah. I think I was hoping he would feel sorry for me and take me with him, but that didn't happen.

The morning he left, we had an argument, and Doug tried to make up for it before saying good-bye. He didn't want us to part on bad terms. But I wasn't willing to forgive, and I was unwilling to tell him what I was feeling for him. I knew he was really leaving me; it was all my fault, and I thought I would die and wished I would. It was difficult being in the same room with Doug because I knew I couldn't change anything between us. He was leaving; I was staying. I was in love with him, but he wasn't. I felt like a fool. I tried to tell him I had taken care of him by doing the laundry, cooking, cleaning, and so on, but he responded with the truth: that all of that was my choice; no one had made me do any of the things I had done for him. The day Doug left for Michigan, I checked myself into the psychiatric unit of Holy Cross Hospital.

I wish my experience with Doug would have taught me a lesson and that nothing like that relationship would have ever happened again. But I made most of the same mistakes once more, this time with a man named Wade. I met him in 1982 when I moved to Tulsa, Oklahoma. The night I met him, I couldn't sleep. It seemed that everything that had happened with Doug went through my head, and I had the premonition that Wade would hurt me in some similar way. But my fascination for Wade was stronger than my fears, and I plunged into another sick relationship.

My sexual feelings were stirred all the time that I was with Wade. He was very handsome and had a fantastic body. I knew I was in love with him. I wanted to have sex with him, and I fantasized about this often. My fantasizing was encouraged with Wade's behavior. He always seemed to need a shower when I came to his apartment, and he made no attempt to be modest. I often wondered if he wanted me to approach him sexually. I suspected that he was confused about his sexuality, but I was afraid that if I told him how I felt about him and if he didn't feel the same way, he would leave me. In my mind that was the worst thing that could possibly happen to me.

I hardly know how to describe my relationship with Wade. In some ways it was one of the most exciting times of my life; he could be more fun than anyone I've ever known. But he also must have recognized how I felt about him, because he could use my vulnerability to hurt me. In the beginning our time alone was spent in intense talking and getting to know each other. Later, Wade decided he couldn't handle those talks, and our time with just the two of us changed. Our time alone usually was a time for me to do his errands or to buy his liquor or food. Gradually, I felt taken for granted and used. Finally, I made a choice; I could no longer allow Wade to walk all over me. It was one of the most difficult decisions I had ever made in my life, but I decided I wasn't going to see him anymore. I couldn't handle my emotions around him any longer, so I went away.

This decision was a long time in the making, however. It took two and a half years before I was able to leave him. During that time, I tried to do everything for him and be everything he needed, and he let me do it all. He began to expect me to take care of him and, after a while, he got tired of me. But Wade never made a clean break from me as Doug had done. He used me to his advantage when he could and avoided me when he didn't want me around.

Because every friend I had in Tulsa I had met through Wade, when I finally stopped seeing him, I stopped seeing almost everyone else I knew, too. I was afraid to socialize because I was afraid to meet Wade and to be around him again. I withdrew completely into my own world. I did have a couple of friends who also felt Wade used people terribly, and they had begun to stay away from him, too. They told me I had done the right thing by leaving, but I didn't feel the closeness with any of them that I had felt with Wade.

In my loneliness I drank daily and was breaking every rule I had ever made about alcohol. Wade and I had gotten drunk and stoned together quite often, but, until the last few months before I left him, I had rarely drank or used pot alone. Now, every night after work I got drunk. Many of my weekends were one long drunk from the time I woke up in the morning, until I passed out somewhere and at sometime during the day.

My drinking years were filled with more times passing out than blacking out. I had a few blackouts, but in most drinking situations I passed out. I passed out often, and it didn't matter where — other people's homes, bars, beaches. I drank to escape, and I liked to pass out. Passing out made the escape ultimate. I couldn't think or feel; I just slept.

I felt incapable of loving or of being loved ever again, and I was lonely and stayed home crying over what I fantasized might have been my relationship with Wade. I was extremely unhappy but afraid to try suicide again. After two previous attempts I believed I had to make the next one count, or I thought that people would accuse me of only trying to get attention, and I was terribly afraid of what people thought of me. The second time I had attempted suicide was while Wade and I were still friends, and he had accused me then of only trying to get attention. I had deeply resented his insensitive remarks. To spite him, I reminded him that he, too, had attempted suicide a year earlier, and I asked if his intention had been only to get attention. He didn't answer me and changed the subject.

My depression eased a little when I stopped pretend-

ing men didn't interest me sexually. All my sexual fantasies were about men, usually Wade. I began to go to adult
bookstores and to buy gay porno magazines, but after a
couple of nights of looking at them I would feel guilty and
throw them away. This went on for quite a while, until one
night in February 1986 when I was in a bookstore; a man
asked me to go home with him, and I did. It was the first
time I had sex with a man, and I knew I had found the answer to my sexual identity....I knew I was gay. It was a relief to admit my sexual orientation and to realize that sex
with a man was enjoyable.

I had sex with a few other men after that first experience, but I wanted to know the feeling of having sex with a
man I really cared about. I finally had that chance with a
man I knew and loved — my friend, Steve. He and I had
been friends for a year before becoming roommates. For
three years, that is all we were to each other, roommates
and friends. I had always thought of Steve as a brother. I
was not obsessive about him, never had sexual fantasies
about him, nor had any sexual desire for him. One night in
September 1986, he and I were stoned, and we started talking about our sexual fantasies. He had also been having
sex with men, but neither of us knew what the other had
been doing. That night he and I had sex with each other
for the first time, and so began the first lover relationship
for both of us.

We had a very difficult time together. Neither of us
knew what we really wanted. We suffered from guilt and
constantly questioned our feelings about being gay. We
decided we needed time away from each other to think
things through. We each went home for Christmas, and,
while we were gone, we thought about what we wanted.

When we returned to Tulsa, we talked for a long time.
We decided that I would go to Oklahoma City on a sched-
uled transfer at the end of January and that Steve would
stay in Tulsa, but that, until then, we would enjoy sex with
each other. The night I left Tulsa was the last time we ever
had sex together, although we've seen each other since.
Steve made a decision to live a straight life; I decided be-

ing gay was natural and normal for me.

I left Tulsa in late January 1987 to start a new life in Oklahoma City, and that is exactly what I've done — started a new life. My first few weeks were difficult; I was drunk all the time and very depressed. In March 1987, I began to seek help from psychologists but was told I had to get help with my drinking before anyone could effectively work with me on sexual and family-related problems. I was at my bottom, emotionally. I was ready to commit suicide again, even though on the surface everything seemed great. I had a new job and a nice place to live, but emotionally, I was a disaster. I was extremely unhappy, lonely and depressed. I wanted out, but I decided I would try to get help with my drinking before making a decision to kill myself.

I went to a treatment center and was told that, along with treatment, I would have to attend meetings of Alcoholics Anonymous. On March 25, 1987, I attended my first A.A. meeting. I stayed sober that entire day for the first time in a long time. Through the fellowship of A.A. and the grace of a loving God (as I understand Him), I have remained sober since that day. I didn't know anything about A.A. when I went to my first meeting, but today I am very grateful I found this program. I am now genuinely happy, and the program is a healthy way of life for me.

In the program I had to work at finding a God of my understanding. In the second step of the program, I came to believe that a power greater than myself could restore me to sanity. But the second and the third steps of the program scared me. I thought I would have to change my gay life in order to stay sober. I didn't talk about being gay in group counseling; I was afraid the other people in the group would not like me if they knew I was gay. But in individual counseling, the therapists I worked with assured me I could be gay and stay sober and still believe that God loved me. Eventually I did find a God of my own understanding, who loves and accepts me as a gay man.

It took time to admit my powerlessness over other people. I still wanted to manipulate others as I had done with Wade and Doug; I still wanted to make people love me. But in the program we learn we have no control over other people. Step eleven tells us to seek knowledge of God's will and the power to carry that out. When I remember to do this, good things happen to me.

In June 1987, I began a relationship with my current lover. He is also an alcoholic, maintaining sobriety one day at a time through the A.A. way of life. I have never had a relationship like the one I enjoy today. I love my man very much, but I don't feel dependent and I don't need to be manipulative in order to keep his love. I enjoy the life we have together on a one day at a time basis.

As I continue to live my life "a day at a time" and to work the steps of the program, I experience a serenity that I never dreamed was possible. I feel so much freedom when I admit the truth about myself and live according to that truth. My life is calm and peaceful; I don't have to be in turmoil to feel alive anymore.

My psychological problems haven't all disappeared, but I've learned that I don't have to act on all of my feelings. I can feel, but action is not always necessary. I may be hurting, but I don't have to scream at people and cry all the time.

Through A.A. and the 12-Step Program, I am discovering the joy of allowing myself to love and to be loved, and not only in my relationship with my lover but also with my many, many A.A. friends. It is my friends in the program who are helping me learn to be happy, joyous and free as a sober gay alcoholic. It's to them that I give my greatest thanks, my thanks to them for being there for me.

12

I Turned to the Steps

Well, here I am again. Another night at Joe's. I was thinking, "Who is it I'm looking for anyway?" I scanned the bar, looked back at my drink and concluded,"Well, it doesn't matter. He isn't here anyway. He doesn't exist."

I'm not surprised that I should have thought that way. He - the man - really didn't exist, except as a dream of that special faceless someone who would come and take me off on his white horse to live with him happily ever after. But I was hardly material for a handsome prince in shining armor. At the end of my (mercifully) short drinking career, I wasn't the new face that could attract attention any more. I probably had had a couple of glasses of white wine (my drink of choice) before I came to the bar to sharpen my wit, and dull my vision. I would have had who knows how many more glasses of white wine during the evening. This happened two or three nights a week, except when I was in one of my dreadful moods, when I would show up at the bar every night. I wasn't looking for sex, at least not directly. No, I was looking for love....love to drive the feelings of inadequacy and worthlessness away. It happened night after night, always the same.

My friend Steve ended up in my apartment one gray February day to talk about business, mainly the affairs of the Dignity chapter (an organization for gay and lesbian Roman Catholics) for which I was secretary and he president. We concluded our business, and I happened to ask why I hadn't seen much of him in the past few months. Since we were close friends, this seemed unusual to me. He responded by telling me what a nice person I had used to be, but that when I drank, all I was was a foul-mouthed bitch. He told me that I was a drunk. He was on a roll and said that there were some things I could do to help myself, but that was my decision. He got in his final punch when he said that if I didn't do anything, I wouldn't see much of him around. That impelled me to attend my first A.A. meeting that same night. Sometimes, bluntness has its place.

I have never been a "normal" drinker. I grew up sheltered from alcohol in a small town in West Michigan. My parents weren't drinkers, at least when I was growing up. (I found out recently that my father was quite a drinker and carouser, though, while he was growing up. When he married my mother, the drinking stopped, but none of the other behavior associated with carousing). My younger brother did all the drinking and carousing in high school, which was more than enough for both of us. I didn't start drinking until I got to college. "Normal" drinkers don't get blasted every time they drink, but I did, which meant that I avoided the opportunity to drink as often as possible.

Ferris State University, where I went to college, was a great party school. The only thing which kept me from drinking was that my friends were eccentric in a '70's sort of way, meaning that we were into white magic and the occult. We created enough mental highs without booze, without other mind-altering chemicals, too, in case you were wondering. I also spent a lot of time denying I was gay. The question of being gay was on a lot of people's minds about themselves for some reason. Ferris wasn't the most liberal of schools, but the question was a continuing issue, nevertheless. I had my first (and only) relationship with a woman during those years. One of my more perceptive friends said that I dated (and almost married) Diane because she was a tom-boy type. He was obviously implying that I was gay, but I continued with the denial. Diane was as nutty as I was at the time, but after a while we broke off our relationship. I initiated the break-up because, since she was a good Catholic who didn't believe in divorce for any reason, I suspected that we would have had a marriage made in hell. After the engagement ended, it became more and more difficult to push my true sexual orientation back into the bottom of the cesspool that my life was becoming.

I came out of the closet in the spring of 1979, with

more of a whimper than a bang. My therapist (straight, but understanding) took one look at my attractions and my depression and, on one March afternoon, broached the subject with me. I came away from the session with the certainty that my being gay had been obvious to everyone but me, the one trapped in denial. I spent the summer trying to figure out what it all meant; in other words I was paralyzed with fear. I finally joined the local Dignity chapter in September, after sitting on the steps of the church where Dignity met for three weeks in a row, afraid to go in. At the chapter's first anniversary dance, I fell in love with a man for the first time.

We dated for a while, but the relationship failed in a rather dramatic way just before Christmas, and just after I had introduced him to my straight friends, who liked him. He was studying to be a priest and wasn't ready for the guilt that resulted from our relationship. We ended our relationship by having a terrific fight on a snowy night driving back from Big Rapids where we had gone to visit some of my college friends. Neither of us knew anything about relationships anyway.

After spending a week of my winter break with my parents in New Mexico, I returned to Lansing to start the new year (1980). Since all areas of my life started to fall apart at once, I grew isolated. I decided that in order to break the depression that I was feeling, I would get more involved in the gay community and get out and meet more people. I continued my involvement with Dignity, becoming secretary of the group. I attended the meetings of the other gay groups in town and, soon, became extensively involved. I was relieved to find that most of the people in the groups were a lot like me. I also found a way to boost my sagging ego, by becoming an officer or by just getting in there and doing the work. I never asked why I wanted to be involved and what paybacks I expected for my efforts.

It was in March 1980 that a friend found out that, even though I was involved in all the gay groups, I had never been to any of the gay bars in town. He set out to remedy this deficiency with a bar tour on my birthday. I date that tour as the time that my drinking really took off. I began drinking so that I could loosen up and talk to people. That motivation soon changed. But, at first, I was still the nice person that Steve talked about. I remember that I used to joke that if I hadn't changed my drink of choice from screwdrivers to wine, I would most certainly have turned into an alcoholic (though I think that by the time I'd switched I already was one). I was a new face at the bar, too, so people took some interest in me from the start, boosting my ego. That also quickly changed.

The rest of the year consisted of my dealing with learning to be a gay man, and of my being involved with the local gay political group as we fought the police harassment in the parking lot across from the bars. I spoke before the Lansing City Council, as we presented our side of the issue, without giving much thought to the fact that I was probably coming out to my family and co-workers in the papers. I ho-hummed the whole matter. I just didn't care too much about the consequences of the actions I took.

This was also the year that I worked hard for the re-election of a local Democratic congressman, only to watch him lose the election. I spent the wee hours of the day after election day on the bathroom floor of the Carter-Mondale headquarters (our headquarters and theirs were in the same downtown hotel), puking my guts out from having drunk too much. This was after I'd had the nerve to cut off a friend, who was the congressman's office manager, before he drank too much. Drinking until I got sick continued to be a problem with me. It happened again at a fundraiser the next year, and again and again. This proved to be embarrassing to me, but did I have a problem with alcohol? No, sir! I couldn't see the pattern that was already setting in. I'm not surprised today that I was depressed all the time then. Even though I never drank every day, the effects of drinking were never really out of my system. It's hard to function when you're hung over all the time.

1981 started out about the same as any other year.

There wasn't too much remarkable about that year, except that my car burned up in August and I continued to drink. Since I spent most of my money on drinking, I didn't do a lot of preventative maintenance on the car, so I wasn't prepared when the seal on the gas line over the manifold gave out and dripped gas, starting a fire. Fortunately, the gas tank was on empty and the damage was confined to the engine. I got the engine repaired, sold the car, and became a pedestrian.

The year ended with one of the worst experiences I ever had. I went to a New Year's Party with friends, became enamored with the host and ended up being the last guest to leave the next morning. I literally tiptoed out of the house; you can fill in the blanks. Two days later, I was drunk from having closed the bar and I slipped on the ice in front of my house; I broke my elbow. This occurred after I'd been turned down for a roll in the hay. I was lucky that I hadn't knocked myself out. It was 10º that night, and I could have froze to death. With my arm in the sling, I continued to go to the bar. Some of my friends were appalled that I was there, but I thought, why stay away.

1982 ended with a bout of hepatitis B that used up all my sick leave at work. It was another fiasco. My doctor was really curious to know how I might have contracted it. I wasn't about to tell. I stopped drinking for a time - doctor's orders - but I resumed in 1983 when my liver returned to normal. I should mention that I have worked for the same employer for the past ten years. Why I wasn't fired during the first five for all my missed days of work I will never understand. I recently learned that, at the time, my colleagues had taken bets on whether I would run out of leave time before another colleague of mine (who, incidentally, did get fired!). Even my sponsor jokes that he couldn't understand why I was promoted at work in 1983, because I was never there!

1983 was the beginning of the end of my drinking. I began to get these hints that I might have a drinking problem. I attended an executive board meeting of Dignity in Atlanta with friends in April. We stayed with friends of theirs, and I'm sure that I wouldn't be welcomed in their house today. I was an embarrassment. They couldn't be sure who would walk out of the bedroom with me in the morning. It was on this trip that I learned that you could depend on a cab driver to get you home, even if you weren't sure of the way because you were too drunk to remember the exact address.

I attended my first A.A. meeting that spring, but I continued to drink. I thought I could handle it. It was only a small problem. I still thought that I was a normal drinker. But do normal drinkers end up with broken elbows, or get lost in strange cities late at night because of their drinking? Or do they go to conventions and stay drunk or hungover for the entire week?

Steve had been invited to present a workshop at Dignity's biennial convention in Seattle. I decided to go along. This wasn't long after Steve had called me excitedly one day to tell me he had gotten a sponsor. It was the first inkling that I had that he had a drinking problem and that he'd gotten into A.A. Then I remembered that not long before this announcement Steve and I had attended a meeting of Dignity/Flint that turned out to be a witnessing by Anne G. and Doug C., who shared what their lives were like before and after choosing sobriety. I thought it was interesting but that it didn't apply to me. Steve found that his life was just like what life had been for them.

The week before Labor Day, we were off to Seattle. We arrived at midnight, and I immediately complained that there was no one there to meet us. Steve ignored me and found the bus that would take us to the hotel from the airport. The hotel had cancelled our reservations and I complained about that. Steve ignored me and worked with the hotel staff to find us a room for the night. It was to be the only sober night I spent in Seattle. The next day we moved to another room, and I was off. Steve could never be sure what he would find when he returned to the room at night. Steve ran A.A. meetings from our room, the "Dry Suite," he called it. Between workshops, I'd clean up the room, pick up the cups, make the coffee, and empty the ashtrays; then when it was time for the meeting, I'd skip out. Steve and I still joke that I was doing Twelve Step work before I needed to. A friend I saw recently, who was also at that convention, doesn't recall much difference in my behavior between the times I was drinking and the times I wasn't. But Steve experienced them and swore that he would never, ever travel with me again.

After the Seattle convention, I began to drop out of the leadership positions I held. Actually, it was a situation that people wouldn't do it my way, so I'd quit, or I was forced aside. I announced at one meeting that since no one else wanted to be president, I would have to be it again. I have never seen such a sudden change of mind, and I had to step aside. It was a miserable experience for me.

Steve's success with the A.A. program and my persistent drinking and obnoxious behavior led to his confrontation with me on that "gray day" of February 8, 1984. It led me to A.A. and a way out of my dead end life. The life I have today is the direct result of working the Twelve Steps in my life...not that I wanted to at first. I was going to A.A. for others, to please them. I tried to continue to live my life in the same way, just not drinking. This led to my having sex with a straight colleague in a local motel and almost being arrested for urinating in public - in the daytime! Incidents like these convinced me that I had to try a different way of living my life, that something had to change. So, I turned to the steps.

It sounds hokey, but the steps worked. I began the process of cleaning house and of healing the past as the steps suggest. By working on that process, I began to have some faith that there was a power greater than I who, with the help of people in A.A., could help me learn to live my life without the need to drink or drug away the problems that were there. I began the process that continues today, of learning how best to fit in the world, rather than of how to make the world fit to my demands.

In the beginning, I used the tools that I had available from my own life but which I'd been neglecting. I used the prayers and the concept of God that I had from my religious background. I soon realized, though, that as long as I wasn't trying to be the higher power in my life, it didn't matter what I thought it was. Today, I don't know whether my idea of God would help anyone else; my concept of the higher power is the life force that is in every living being. I get the answers I need through prayer and meditation and from the people of A.A., who have the uncanny ability to speak the words I need to hear. Also, the discipline of the program was especially valuable when I was first beginning A.A.

I learned how to be a co-worker at work, learning how to carry the full load that I was expected to. I learned that work can be a lot more pleasant when you aren't fighting with your co-workers all the time, or involved in the train of gossip that can travel around any work-place. I figure I have about another year and a half of time to make up to my employer, so I show up for work when I am supposed to, do my job and try to do the best work I can.

I learned to bear the pain of life and not to drink or to use drugs. My father died suddenly in January 1985 of a heart attack. That started a string of losses that continued for most of that year. My supervisor at work (who had promoted me), a friend just at the beginning of his career, his mother, just one person after another. The relationship that I had started at seven months of sobriety also failed. But I learned about the unconditional love that is everywhere in A.A. Even in the midst of all the pain, I was able, with the help of fellow members of A.A., to see that the strength and love was available for the asking. A.A also helped to teach me the value of living in the now, this day, these twenty-four hours...to live in the present to the fullest and in the best way that we can. Today, if I think of calling someone, I call him. If I want to visit a person, I visit him or her. I remember not to take for granted anyone in my life, since that person's presence in my life is a gift, that can be withdrawn at any time.

I learned the difference between having a friend and being one, and the difference between wanting to be loved and making myself a lovable person. Through the steps, I gained the self-love and self-respect that allow me to treat myself better today. A.A allowed me the chance to learn how to trust people again, especially gay people. I was able to get rid of my own self-hatred, the thing that always was this little voice in the back of my head that said, "you are unlovable; you are unworthy; you have to settle for less."

I met my current partner at an A.A. meeting in December 1985. We began our relationship slowly, learning more about each other and about how to be a couple and still work a separate program. We moved in together and began to join our lives in June 1986. We continue to work together and to stay together. We are the only gay male couple in the program in our area. Since there are only three gay meetings a week in Lansing, we have to reach out to all A.A. groups. In all of them, - gay or straight - we act as if everyone already knows that we are a couple. It saves the hassle of having to explain. The freedom we have because of that decision is worth the small cost. Learning how to trust straight people was a big issue for me in the beginning. But, as I went to meetings, I learned and continue to learn that while the specific situations are different, the feelings that are there are really much the same. I really believe that most straight people in A.A. are ignorant of gay folk, rather than being bigoted. The only way that they can learn about us is if they see us in meetings and if we are involved in service. We can also help assure that tolerance is maintained in A.A. by being around to confront people when they try to talk negatively about gay people. There are five or six people I can think of in the meetings that I attend regularly who are dealing with sexuality issues. I can be there for them, too. Besides, I need all points of view on the steps and on how to work them - the best reason not to exclude myself from straight meetings. It really didn't matter in the beginning who it was that was showing me the way; I needed a guide, plain and simple, and no one ever turned me away.

I guess that's the most important thing for me today. No one turned me away, no one forced me to tow an ideology line or to be of a certain sexual orientation. My sponsors have become my trusted friends, to the point that we really sponsor each other. The healthy life I have today is a direct result of learning to depend on others and to ask for help to stay sober one day at a time. Not drinking a day at a time has proved to be the gateway to freedom and the road to a sane and more serene life. No one in A.A. turned me away from this.

13

Sandy

My name is Sandy. For one day at a time, I have been sober in Alcoholics Anonymous since November 5, 1974. I live in Baltimore in a row house near the baseball park. My home is shared with a significant other friend, not really a lover, but a man I care about a great deal who has been my partner for five years. He is the second man I have met, since being sober, that I have shared my life with in an affectionate, sometimes sexual, close and loving way. I have called these relationships ones of "two orphans in a storm," not being aware of A.C.O.A. (Adult Children of Alcoholics) when I named them. A.C.O.A. applies to my life and the lives of the two men who have lived with me. The devastation of alcoholism was a storm robbing me of parental love and direction and claiming me to continue in its whirlpool of self-centered depression and doubt.

I grew up on a hill in Maryland country during the 1950's when suburban sprawl was changing the shape of my surroundings. My family's white, middle class, Irish Catholic status contrasted starkly to the status of the "colored folk" living along the railroad tracks in shacks with outhouses. We lived in big old house with woods all around us and views of rivers from both ends of the party room. The colored Casbar that I would pass on the track whenever I vowed to run away from home fascinated me. It was a nightclub that always seemed to be busy. But I didn't have to go past the Casbar to see a lot of partying; our home was often a nightclub itself with dancing, drinking, and laughter filling the house till dawn.

Haunting events, however, clouded memories of good times, and for most of my life I've been victim to the storm I remember. My father let my younger sister play with his penis when she was five; I was six. It left me feeling excluded and deprived, and with a strange sense of what was sexual. At ten I tried to take my life by overdosing on a couple of bottles of pills. Shortly after that, on a New Year's Eve, I was sent out for ice in the snow. I slipped on the way to the neighbors' and came back crying, iceless and upset. My father, drunk and probably in a blackout, struck me and knocked me across the room. Shortly after that incident, I remember that we moved to the New Jersey coast. I was sent to a Christian Brothers' Academy. I was a physically awkward, sensitive, shy, freckled flaming redhead with baby fat about the chest who knew already that he was different and who felt like a failure compared to his well-hung, extroverted Black Irish rogue of a father.

Someone on the bus the first day of school gave me the nickname, Sally, which stuck with me as a stigma, depriving me of self-confidence and a secure sense of masculinity. Then my father died. I turned to the sea, a block from our house, as a source of strength and romance. Whatever sense of God I might have had felt from the sea got drowned and was washed away when alcohol, other drugs, and sex became my higher power. But before turning to alcohol, I had my first adult same-sex sexual experience with a passive, indifferent partner that confirmed for me that I was neither a man nor someone capable of being loved. I tried suicide again. My stomach was pumped. My mother, whose existence seemed to depend as much on denial as mine did on escape, gained my agreement to remain silent about what had happened. The note I wrote disappeared.

This is when booze entered the picture for me. To survive, I needed a goal, one to confirm my manhood and to conceal my homosexuality. I decided to study hard, to go to college and law school, to enter the military and take care of my "duty," to marry someone rich, to run for public office and to become President of the United States. Alcohol served as a suppressant of my sex drive and a cover for my deep insecurity and sadness. This is not to say that the conditions I've described caused my alcoholism: I firmly believe that I was predisposed to the disease and that drinking triggered the addiction, along with its symptom of denial (including the rationalization and justification system or web of lies set up to defend my alcoholism).

I got as far as law school with drinking progressively increasing and getting me into trouble. I did not know that drinking was a problem at that time, or I wasn't able to honestly acknowledge the connections until I came to A.A. Blackouts, a drunk and disorderly arrest, a broken foot, a car wreck, a growing reliance on the bottle and a need for greater quantities to achieve the needed effects allowed me to hide and escape and repress my sexual desire. My binge drinking became daily drinking, and where my drinking would lead me each day became more and more unpredictable. Until the day I came to A.A., I called alcohol the "glue that kept me together," preventing me from killing myself. The booze intake was interrupted only by experimenting with drugs in 1969 and 1970. Hallucinogens and the cultural revolution of the 1960's established a break with my past.

On LSD (lysergic acid diethylamide), my homosexuality was thrown onto a screen projected in distorted ways for all the world to see. Desire and consciousness of that desire filled me. I could no longer deny my sexual orientation or outlaw status in America. I came out after first going through my first withdrawal. The drugs had replaced booze in my life, and there was not a day that I did not consume something to get high or come down or to get going when I needed to study. After a year's use in isolation filled with paranoia, having the shakes and sweats, being insomniac, and having audio and visual hallucinations, I stopped all the drugs. I was unable to make routine, simple decisions and was constantly on the verge of tears. In that state I stopped into the school health clinic and asked for an exam. They strongly urged me to see a psychiatrist. I began therapy, which included trying to accept my homosexuality, while working and going to school and returning to alcohol.

When I left law school and therapy, I had accepted my status as a gay man, but not as a sexual person or someone for whom love and romance were possible. The stigma of "Sally," the distorted image of sex gotten from seeing my father and sister and from my feeling left out, the rejection I felt from my first partner, the sense that sex was dirty, secret and unconnected with love, and the abandonment I felt when my father had died, all seemed to bury any positive picture of erotic imagery. I sought sex in dark, dirty, dangerous places where anonymity was pretty much the rule, and the possibility of punishment by vice cop arrest was always present. I could not accept myself as eligible for anything more.

At the same time, I threw myself into gay liberation politics. I became close to a martyr working for other people's freedom from oppression, while denying my own shame, self-hatred, and imprisonment. At a meeting of gay activists, I met Cade. He was president of the group. Cade was calm and courageous. He had something I admired and wanted. I learned it was sobriety and serenity. He let me know that he was a recovering alcoholic and that he had helped to start the first gay A.A. meeting in the city (Washington, D.C.). He was the first person I confided in that I thought I might have a drinking problem. He gave me the booklet *20 Questions*. I took the test and failed miserably. Within a week or two I was at my first A.A. meeting, and two nights later I attended my first gay A.A. meeting - a Step group on Capitol Hill. My second period of withdrawal began.

The hardest parts were learning to like myself, to feel that I deserved recovery, and to develop a relationship with a higher power. My acceptance of a God was complicated not only by my involvement in gay liberation politics (which was then basically anti-religious) but also by my adopting Marxist-Leninist theory as a guide to understanding the world and shaping my actions. The God of my childhood and youth was connected with organized religion and its condemnation of same-sex sexual activity. The notion that a higher power's will for me was to be happy, joyous, and free contradicted the ideas of sinner/saint and heaven/hell that I was told to believe in. Also, Marx had described religion as a tool of oppression by the ruling class. However, I knew deep down inside that I needed a God to survive, and I came to believe in a higher power for myself that transcended Roman Catholicism and dialectical materialism. I told my friends on the Left that I would rather be alive and full of contradictions than a dead purist.

Getting sober with healthy gay men and lesbians who accepted and exhibited a spiritual awakening gave me courage and hope to pursue prayer and meditation with my own concept of a loving God. Getting sober in A.A. taught me patience and tolerance I had never had before. I could be friends with men and women the same age as my parents. I got a sponsor old enough to be my grandfather. A whole new world was opening up for me, and I was developing a new vision. I began applying the principles of the program in all my affairs, or maybe I should say some of them. I made progress in my career. I developed important relationships, gay and straight, including my first close relationship with another man which was affectionate as well as sexual. On weekends we would drive to West Virginia to stay with his parents, stopping along the way to walk in the mountains or along a river. On my A.A. anniversary, he baked me a cake. Our relationship was not ideal, but it was a significant gift of companionship helping to sustain and enrich my early sobriety. I had someone special in my life, someone I could instinctively trust. In all areas of my life, save one, I was seeing the "promises" of Alcoholics Anonymous come true. In my sex life, however, I was stuck in a vicious cycle which was taking on a life of its own, crippling me spiritually and bringing me to an emotional crisis and bottom once again.

Five years sober, I left D.C. and moved to Baltimore. In the back of my mind, I thought things would be different, sexually. The move, partially motivated by the desire to take a geographic cure, was, looking back, a good one for me. I threw myself into A.A., exercised daily, and changed my lousy eating habits. I began writing regularly, something that still brings me deep personal satisfaction. I also matured politically and accomplished a lot, including organizing a gay and lesbian political club and serving as an officer of a fledgling gay community center. I even formed a significant bond with a second man, but continued to compulsively cruise and to engage in ritualized, degrading, anonymous, and, often, public sex. The AIDS crisis and the response by the gay community calling for safe sex and for knowing your partner(s) forced me to admit my powerlessness. Also, when people talked in A.A. meetings about alcoholism, I heard them describing my relationship to sex. Fear of spiritual bankruptcy, as much as a fear of AIDS or police arrest, led me to cry out for help by calling a famous sexologist at John Hopkins Hospital.

At my initial visit, I opened up by describing in detail what it was like for me, and, for the first time in memory, I talked about the incident involving my father and sister. Not knowing the Big Book was being quoted, this therapist said that with help and effort it might be possible for me to know "a new freedom." I felt that my higher power was talking to me through somebody else, and I became willing to turn over the care of my life and will at that moment. A therapy and treatment program began, and I was encouraged to organize a self-help group, which I did. It was called the Compulsive Cruisers' Support Group, and it has been meeting for close to three years on every Monday night in the Health Clinic of the Baltimore Lesbian and Gay Community Center just before the gay meeting of A.A. The group is described as sex-positive and gay-affirmative to differentiate it from sexual compulsive groups that are often sex-negative and homophobic. Each gay man must determine what he wants to change and how to define his sexual "sobriety" using the 12 Steps. The group views the problem of compulsive cruising more like one of overeating, rather than like the alcoholic's allergy to alcohol. Although the goal of A.A., Overeaters' Anonymous, and Compulsive Cruisers is to help the individual achieve a higher quality of life, one basic strategy is different for A.A. versus overeating and compulsive cruising, that is, unlike the total abstinence from alcohol called for by A.A., O.A. and Compulsive Cruisers do not require total abstinence from food or sex, respectively, to achieve the goal of an increased quality of life. Indeed, Compulsive Cruisers calls for celebrating sex by using it wisely (based on rational planning) to achieve a better quality of life.

This withdrawal for me was the most painful period of my life. I had withdrawn from alcohol, other mind-altering drugs, sugar, and nicotine, but this stripped me naked emotionally. I threw myself into working the Steps again. The memories of growing up that I had hoped could be left behind me and forgotten had to be reconsidered. I disengaged from political activity, retreated to get to know myself better, and went through six months of sustained and deep depression. Slowly, I came out of the abyss a new man, able to integrate sex into my life without shame and without feeling I had to hide things. A catharsis came for me in the summer of 1986 when I dated a man in a gay A.A. group, got erotically involved and fell in love for the first time in my life. This experience left me without a sexual compulsion. It also gave me a new basis on which to imagine sex, as part of relating to someone to whom I was attracted and whom I'd get to know and let know me. To have this happen at the age of 40 was something I was both embarrassed about and grateful for. I was going through what usually happens to people in their teens. So, too, for the first time in my life, I went through lovesickness and being heartbroken after the man I loved rejected me. For months I cried every day. I lost 20 pounds. I could have easily lost faith and hope, given up and ended my life. But, through a miracle of love, I survived. The love that kept me going was not just what was inside me, but was also the love I got from and shared with my other "orphans in the storm," my A.A. sponsor, my counselors, my friends inside and outside of A.A., and the Compulsive Cruisers' Support Group. My heterosexual counselor, A.A. friends, and sponsor had shown me there were men and women outside of gay groups of A.A. I could trust. At the same time, I learned I needed the special support found in gay groups, groups in which I could develop skills for relating, dating, and bonding. In such groups, I could find a special sense of fellowship and intimacy and be a big brother or just a good friend.

My life is rich today. Besides working at a professionally challenging and satisfying job, I swim every morning a mile and a half, do the 12 Steps, do service work in A.A. and Compulsive Cruisers' Support Group, maintain a home with my special friend, write and publish regularly in a gay newspaper, spend as much time as possible close to nature near woods and water, pray and meditate, and enjoy the company of myself and friends. Through writing, I've become politically active again, more now as a consciousness-raiser than as an organizer and hell-raiser. I've come to terms with and forgiven my parents. My 9th Step (making amends) with my dad, who has been dead for over twenty years, came in a dream. In it we accepted each other, to the best of our abilities, as we are (or were) with our faults and our powerlessness over much that we did or did not do.

Last November, when I wondered whether I could survive being hopelessly in love without any chance of that love being reciprocated, I found spiritual sustenance in music. While listening to Richard Strauss' Death and Transfiguration, a surrender of sorts came over me, sufficient enough to put my pain into the words of a poem. For me the poem expresses shared recovery and vulnerability. I would like to end my story with this poem, a prayer, really, of a soul in search of love and peace; a prayer prayed with the awareness that in life and sobriety there will be, must be, joy, struggle, and surrender.

Sandy

Call him Sandy, worn shell of a man,
thrown back by the sea a seasoned creature,
basking in the sun,
waiting to be wondered at and touched.

Windswept, aged, strengthened,
Sandy left his shell
a muscular, lean, athletic

lover of men and friend of women,
unafraid to show the world
his pain, tears, soft spots or desires.

Sandy survived the storm
with its waves of defeat,
currents of fear and doubt
and an undertow of confusion and indecision.

Sandy surfaced breathless, fatigued but alive
and reached for the love of another sailor
lost at sea;
They, together, licked each other's salt and foam
and rode the wind with waves of bliss
on a shaky raft.

Matt moved away as quickly as he had come
out of the clouds and shadows
cast back into long darkness.

Sandy wept alone in a whirlpool
unable to fathom the will of the gods,
knocked about and tossed ashore
against moonlight, confused,
in misery and despair.

Barefoot on cold sand along silent unassuring shores
Loneliness, unlike any loneliness he had ever known,
filled him and he cried out:
Gentleness filled him,
a gentleness he had not seen before,
and in grief he shared his soul
with the weary, lonely, beached
who told Sandy their tales of shipwreck, drowning
and great loss.

Fathoming tenderness as a breaker against the cruel
sea
was new to Sandy,

riding the waves without struggle, confident from sur-
render;
Broken-hearted survivor without a shell
Sandy swims, often sad, but at last, calm and free.

14

"You Are My Beloved"

I'm Larry, and I'm an alcoholic. I'm also gay. I've come to believe that the former has to do with a disease, and that the latter does not. I did not arrive at this conclusion easily.

I first went to A.A., about four years ago. At that time, I owned a condominium and held a job that paid in the top quarter of national incomes. My "bottom" [the event or period immediately preceding and leading to one's choosing sobriety] was not "low" [characteristic of the skid-row, derelict drunk]. True, I had miniature liquor bottles stashed in my desk, my glove compartment, and my brief case against the possibility that I might have to meet someone and talk to him. Liquor would somewhat allay my panic of dealing with people. But I usually chose to stay by myself at home, never feeling good enough about myself to deal with the world outside unless fortified by alcohol.

I would have said I was a "periodic drinker" [a drinker whose intoxications occur intermittently, such as binge drinking]. But, in fact, the periods were getting closer and closer together, and I seldom was able to drink without getting drunk, no matter what my resolve. I would resolve not to drive drunk, then end up doing so. I was protected somehow. I was never pulled over, and I never struck anyone.

When I went to my first A.A. meeting at the A-T Center in Los Angeles, I had resolved to accept my role as a pariah. I knew virtually nothing of other gay men on a social basis, so when I saw twenty or so gay men in the room, I thought, When's the group sex? When do we strip? I knew the thought was not appropriate, but my main previous associations with gay men were in bath houses and tea rooms [public toilets].

Since that first A.A. meeting, I've gotten over much of

my shame about being gay, thanks to a gay psychologist I'd gotten into therapy with about a year after my wife left me. After about one year of therapy, he told me, "When you get up in the morning, ask someone for help."

I was incensed. I shot back, "Warren Beatty?!" I'd always had a passionate devotion for men of that sort and assumed my life would have been complete if only I could have enticed one of them to "marry" me. But ask God for help?! I was far too intelligent and well educated to believe in superstitious nonsense like that. And my shrink should have known that. Later I told him, "Do you know how tenuous our bond became at the moment you made that suggestion?"

He replied, "Did you notice it was a year before I did so?" He said I was an alcoholic and that I should go to A.A. So, in my case, I paid for my own "Eskimo." [A.A. has a story about a man freezing to death in the Arctic wastes who prayed to God for help. God told the man He would save him. An Eskimo came by offering to help, and the man said, "No, thank you, God Himself said He would save me." The Eskimo went his way, and the man froze to death. The man was quite angry when he met his creator, accusing Him of going back on His word. "But," said God, "I sent you an Eskimo." The story illustrates a widely held belief that God works through people to accomplish His ends.]

My beloved shrink also encouraged a sexual relationship that had started in a "tea room." The relationship was with a man I knew slightly prior to the sexual encounter. He and I were both afraid of AIDS, so we developed a monogamous sexual relationship which lasted until four months after I joined A.A. At that point, I entrapped a man of one year's sobriety into moving his two-bedroom-houseful of belongings into my condo...and himself into my double bed. He and I had met at an A.A. meeting, and we began to date like "normal" folk. I was sure that this was at last my long awaited male lover. Seventy-eight days later, he tearfully rejected me sexually, and I fled the room and fell to my knees chanting, "Thy will, not mine, be done." It was the only thing I could remember of my program. I chanted it over and over like a mantra. The pain, miraculously, lifted. I think it was a "spiritual experience."

I had had other spiritual experiences before this. The earliest occurred shortly before I went to my first A.A. meeting. One evening I stood in circle of gay men, including a gay Roman Catholic priest, and listened to the priest say, "Whenever any two or three of you are gathered in my name, I'll be there." It was a Mass in the home of a man I'd met at a bath house. I attended the service not out of any religious sentiment, but only out of a sense of social obligation. However, those words suddenly filled me with relief and joy. I felt a loving God in the room. I felt the same presence later, at my first A.A. meeting. God, the loving protector, had come into my life. And I have since come to see that it was only my willingness that was necessary to perceive it. He had been there all along.

The sexual rejection was difficult for me. The desire to dispel the heartache with drink was strong. Somehow I chose sobriety and the tools of the program, probably because they, too, worked to relieve pain. Part of that pain, of course, was my fear that I would never again have a lover; this man was my "last chance," I thought. We were both in our 50's then.

After he left, I did some bath house sex again, but it was different in sobriety. I think that I knew I was desiring for a "fix" when what I really needed was spiritual growth. The shrink was useful during this time in getting me through the pain and keeping me glued to A.A. He encouraged my getting back together with the first man, for sexual safety. We did resume that relationship, and we're still together. I like something he said to me recently, "You know...I'm not in love with you, but I do love you." It's the way I feel about him, too.

We've taken the HIV antibody test twice, six months apart, to confirm that we are both negative, and we maintain a sexually monogamous relationship. Concern for preserving my own health has forced monogamy on my life.

Monogamy is something I thought I didn't want, but now I enjoy it. In these ways we're each protecting his own health, and there has been an unexpected bonus. For me, the commitment to protect one another against AIDS has increased my admiration of him and my respect for myself. I like what I feel about him. It's a feeling at several levels, summarized in the single word, "love."

I had been monogamous with my wife. Monogamy became total abstinence in the last years of our marriage. I felt very guilty about that. When she left, she also felt guilty about deserting me. I may have mitigated some of her guilt by telling her I was gay. Much as I hated the separation, I now look upon it as the start of a new life. It's not just that my new life gives me the sort of sex I want; it's that I experience a downright deep sense of joy, of living a life that is honest and caring.

My coming out roughly parallels my sobriety. The first year of my sobriety I was afraid to attend the Gay Pride Parade in West Hollywood for fear someone I knew would see me in the audience. The next year, I saw friends going by in the parade and wished I could have been with them. And the third year I marched with them, as part of the AIDS Project "Buddy" group. Many of them were gay A.A.'s like myself. I was very proud of the people I was with and of the people along the parade route who shouted their support. One group in the audience had those little cards numbered 1 through 10, and they were grading the hunks as they went by on the floats. As we very ordinary men and women buddies marched by, they held up their grades for us: 10, 10, 10, 10, 10, 10... My eyes stung with happy tears at the sight.

I fled at the end of the parade because I could smell the beer at the carnival. The memory of that event is indelible. I know that I felt myself a pariah among pariahs; I was a drunk and gay. Later, attending A.A. support meetings for persons with AIDS, I thought, Am I now a pariah among pariahs among pariahs? And I felt God answer; "No, you are my beloved, and you are at the Holy of Holies."

The parade helped me believe that the whole gay community senses the same thing, a love we have discovered for one another in the face of calamity. Our detractors may consider AIDS to be a judgment against us. The truth we have found is that it is turned by a loving God into a spiritual opportunity to express the love within us. That's quite some trip for a man who four years ago resented the notion of being told to call on a Higher Power for help....and for one who was full of fear that he might be suspected of being gay.

Being gay is a gift. I have sometimes rolled my eyes at heaven and said sarcastically, "Thanks a lot!" as some new trial is sent in the direction of the gay community or at me personally. But, in my opinion, God does that. Something that looks like a burden is really a gift.

At this time in my life, I can honestly say that I've never been happier. The gay men and lesbians that I know and love number in the hundreds. My sexual activity is confined to my monogamous relationship. I neither regret the past nor wish to relive it.

I'm not especially comfortable going to non-gay A.A. meetings yet. When I go, I find myself feeling judgmental, bored, constrained, even threatened. It's mostly in my mind, I know. I wish I felt otherwise, and I believe my attitude will change. My beloved shrink said to me, "Most people tend to accept us in direct proportion to our acceptance of ourselves. And all gays are homophobic to some degree." Once again, I can deal with the problems I have with "them" by dealing with my own attitudes. I hope to continue to grow and expect one day to feel free to share fully in a non-gay meeting.

15

Lost Paradise

I've always known that I was gay. But growing up in the 40's, I was confused and bewildered, as I wanted to be accepted by the attractive and popular girls...the cheer leader type was my real "bag", but deep down I was always looking for a cute guy to take me into the boy's bathroom to give me a blow job. Actually, this happened to me in high school one afternoon after swim practice. I never could understand whether I liked being on the team to swim or for having the many opportunities of being in the locker room with lots of nude guys from all the different high schools all over Chicago.

The first time I "popped" was when I was between 12 and 13. It was one beautiful sunny afternoon in the summer of '47 or '48. It was with Billy, one of my best friends. He now has three children, as do I. I spent a few days with him and his second wife recently when I was on my way to my son's graduation from Navy boot camp. Billy has not changed much over the years, but there is no mention of our little get together during our talks about old times.

My drinking began the summer between my junior and senior years of high school. I even remember the occasion at which I took my first drink; it was at a beach party in Chicago that I was attending with my "true love," Judy. I believed that Judy and I were in love. My mother believed Judy was taking advantage of me because Judy insisted that I buy her cashmere sweaters for her birthdays and for Christmas as proof of my love for her. Mother thought it was unnecessary and silly to spend so much money on a girl that I would never see again, since Judy was going to the University of Colorado and I was going to Illinois. Little did my mother know that I was planning on Colorado as well, and that's where we both went as freshmen in the fall of 1953. By this time, I was a full bloom drunk...beers all the time....hard liquor sometimes.

After we arrived in Boulder, I saw Judy about three times in the two years I attended the university, as she met a nice guy from Juneau, Alaska, married him and, as far as I know, is still up there with him. MOTHER WAS RIGHT...Judy was a gold digger in more ways than one.

I flunked out of school....too much partying. Billy was at Boulder, too, and for a few months I lived with him and a few guys, but I had my little drunken meetings with a couple of other guys who liked to get it on sexually. Maybe it was the booze or maybe they were really gay, I don't know. What I knew about myself, however, was getting really drunk and very hot. The drunker I got the more I searched out sex. I remember waking up in a number of motel rooms outside of Boulder with guys who were total strangers. They would drive me back to my apartment, where I'd drown my loneliness in a lot of beers and go on another search.

In 1955 I moved back to Chicago and became involved in the world of advertising. What a mistake! Little did I know that alcohol was a very integral part of the daily life of an advertising man. Who knew that the double and triple martini lunches were to become as important to me as breathing, and that repeatedly I would wake up with a hangover in some stranger's near-north-side-of-Chicago penthouse apartment. I was a very attractive number in those days and very fun to be with. I loved to stay in the all night gay bars of Chicago and trick out whenever possible.

Then, I got to know Bob, my manager in the research department, at a Christmas party which we had at a downtown hotel and which he hosted. He had made a reservation to stay overnight at the hotel. I was too drunk to catch the Illinois Central to the south side of Chicago, where I still lived with my parents, so Bob suggested that I just sleep on the couch of his hotel room and then go to the office from there the next day. Well, we became instant lovers.

Bob and I became a rather sensational "item." In the first place, he was fifteen years older than I. He soon divorced his wife with whom he had two kids. Then he was transferred to the New York office because he was too good to let go, but our relationship had become common knowledge to the big guys in the corner offices who believed it was just not what was acceptable...a cute, young research assistant and a vice-president of the second largest ad agency in the world living together. This was in 1957.

January 1960 found us living in Greenwich Village. Bob was still a VP with the same company, but New York seemed to offer a larger capacity than Chicago for the antics of two gay guys living together and drinking at least a fifth of bourbon a night. In 1961 I started running around with my wife-to-be and drinking great quantities of liquor to escape the guilt I felt at the fact that I was living with my lover, Bob, but fooling around with Nancy because she had a lot of money. Nancy was working for one of my clients and was extremely attractive. My sister died very unexpectedly in November 1961. I married Nancy in June 1962. People have asked me why. My reasons (probably unconscious at the time) were that I wanted to replace my sister for my parents and that I was a drunk and had lost control of myself.

Our honeymoon at St. Thomas led to many interesting consequences. We took a position as a hotel manager couple and quit our good jobs in New York to live in the tropics. After two months of marriage, my love life consisted of sleeping with anyone on the island who was willing to take me home. One day I staggered up to the hotel office to inquire after the whereabouts of my wife and the owners looked at their watches and said that she was probably somewhere between Long Island and Maryland. They had put her on a plane to NYC that morning. I was left with no money, no job and no place to live. I called up one of my tricks, and he said I could move in for a few days until I could get myself together and get off the island. I took advantage of his hospitality for two months before I finally had the strength to get home. During those two months I still drank at least a 1/2 gallon of liquor a day - mostly Beefeaters gin straight out of the bottle. I think I have the disreputable distinction of being the only white man to have ever slept in the street in front of Katie's. For any of you who knew St. Thomas in the '60's, you would have to have been to Katie's. I have often considered going back to St. Thomas just to see what it is like and, especially, to sit down in the street in front of Katie's where I was a real drunken bum!

Why did I become alcoholic? What triggered my need for booze? Was my mother an influence over my alcoholism, over my homosexuality? I have recently become involved with the Forum, a Werner Erhard EST program. For me, it has opened up a great deal of what life is all about and why people are who they are. I know now that my mother was an influence on me, just as mothers all over the world are the primary influences on their children, but that they should not be blamed for all the outcomes. People basically are who they are because they choose to be the persons they are, at least that's how I understand it. I liked beer...gin...booze of any kind, and I chose to drink it. I'd have had a tough time with vermouth at 8:00 a.m; but if there had been nothing else to drink and there were 30 inches of snow on the ground and my car were buried and the liquor store weren't open and I had no money anyway, I'd have chosen to drink the vermouth! I got married because I chose to. My wife and I had children because we wanted them. I continued to drink because my body required alcohol, but it was my choice to satisfy that need. I am gay because there's nothing wrong with being gay. I've also chosen to be a sober alcoholic, and I love it. I am afraid that my present lover, who is alcoholic, will have to hit the bottom before he realizes that he has a problem. I love him, and I choose to continue to live with him. But I will never allow myself to consider myself a co-alcoholic because of his choice to be a drunk. We are both human beings, and we have chosen this relationship. Some of my friends say that, if I were to leave him, he would "shape up." This is nonsense. This is their conception of "my problem." If I do not have a problem with his alcoholism, then it really is "their problem."

My three children and I have a relatively good relationship at this time. Peter is twenty-three and just as straight as they come, but he is alcoholic and has been in A.A. To the best of my knowledge, he still has too much to drink occasionally. My twenty-one year old daughter, Kristin, is married to a user in Texas. She has been known to snort a little coke, and I've heard that she does or has done crack. But she tells me that all is okay on the drug scene now. Then there is Molly. She is eighteen and claims to be alcoholic, but I have always felt that this is just play acting. They have known for years now that I am gay and alcoholic. Incidentally, Molly is now in the Army and my ex-wife thinks Molly is lesbian. Wonderful, I say!

My life is wonderful, now that I am free of booze. I have not had even as much as lobster newburg with a drop of sherry in it for about 14 years. I feel very comfortable with my business career and with my social life. The society I keep is mixed with gay groups, straight people and my clients (some of whom realize I am gay and feel very comfortable with my sexual orientation). I am active to an extent in my community with the human rights issues of the day.

I am thankful that I stopped drinking. I know that if I hadn't stopped on Labor Day of 1975, I would be dead by now. I know that if I hadn't stopped smoking in the fall of 1976, I would have lung cancer or emphysema now. I know that if I had fought my homosexuality, I would have continued drinking and smoking.

This is the essence of my story. I think it speaks to many gay and straight people. To those who have chosen sobriety, it means they can rejoice with me; to those who have not, I hope it can mean that they have further encouragement to begin their own story of choosing sobriety.

16

It's Worth It

My message is one of hope. My name is Josh, and I'm an alcoholic. (I feel as if I were at a meeting!) I had a choice whether to use my real first name, and I decided not to. The hard part was choosing the new name for myself. It's nice to have a choice, but sometimes I still find it very hard to make simple choices. I came up with some interesting names, but Josh seems to feel right as a nickname for me. (Believe me, I've had other nicknames, if you know what I mean.)

I was born and raised in the South - Atlanta, Georgia to be exact. Yes, I am a Southern boy. I really am a man now, but when I joined A.A. six years ago, at age twenty-five, I did not feel like a man; I felt like a boy. Today, after much growth in this wonderful A.A. program, I am beginning to feel like a young man.

When I was growing up, my mother was alcoholic, and I told her I would never be like her. Today, I realize I am almost a carbon copy of her in many respects. I have learned "never to say never" because everytime I do, I end up eating my words.

I am one of those who will tell you that, as far back as I can remember, I always felt different, and that, for a long time I felt alone in feeling different. Now, of course, I know I am not the only one who felt this way growing up, and I don't feel alone anymore in feeling that I'm different. I also thought my childhood was the worst, until I heard the stories of others who grew up with an active alcoholic in the family.

My mother was the alcoholic in the family, and my father was the workaholic. Being raised up by an alcoholic is something I would not wish on my worst enemy, if I had one. It meant a lot of sleepless nights and a lot of fear in my early years. I remember going to elementary school and my friends would be talking about what fun their families had had over the weekend. I would shiver, thinking about the yelling and screaming that went on in my family. I was the odd man out at school. I was one of the last picked for ball teams, and I felt extremely uncomfortable around other boys. For four years, I went to a Catholic school. When I was in the fourth grade, I was caught "experimenting" with another boy in the church bathroom. That was the first time I was told I was going to hell, and I was always afraid of God after that. Soon after that incident, I learned I could escape in books and music. I joined the band and was able to stay away from my house a little longer each day. This was the beginning of how I learned not to feel. I have always known I was a sensitive person and have never liked it, until now. Today I use my sensitivity in many areas of my life to my benefit.

I was very young when I realized that I liked boys, not girls, and this added to my other feelings of being different as a youngster. As I approached adolescence, I embarked on a ten year journey of trying to "fit in." During this period of my life, with the help of my mother and my church, I learned many things about guilt, and not always without justification. I was the bad kid in the family...rebellious is a mild description. I lied and cheated, and I stole from everyone. I was very egocentric and nothing mattered but me. Still, I had no sense of self, and my self-esteem was based on what others thought of me. As a result, and despite my often bad behavior, I ranked among the world's greatest people pleasers. This is an aspect of my personality that I still work on constantly.

I had my first drink at age fifteen. From day one I drank to get drunk. I threw up a lot at first, but that did not stop me. I have never been able to "socially drink." I can't even conceive what that would be like. Once I started drinking and doing other drugs, I found that I instantly "fit in" and that all my troubles seemed to disappear. I ran around with a group that stayed high all day. We would meet in the mornings before high school classes started and drink and do drugs. I would drink a quart of beer and smoke some pot or use some other drug. Then at lunch I would sneak off and try to keep my buzz going. This went on through my senior year. Alcohol helped me to relax, and I discovered I did not feel so shy anymore. This stuff was the answer to all my problems. I ended up being involved in many campus activities and was even elected President of the student body. What an example I must have been!

When I was sixteen, I went to my first gay bar. Don't ask me how I got in because I know I did not look a day over fourteen. I am sure the fact that I slept with the doorman had nothing to do with it! Let me tell you, when I found out that all gay men were not wrinkled old perverts, I was in heaven. I remember thinking that I was going to go out every might for the rest of my life. Believe me, I tried. I couldn't wait to graduate from high school so I could move out and party. During this time my family did an intervention on my mother, and she decided to join A.A. (She has been a member ever since and will be celebrating her fourteenth anniversary this year.) This was my first exposure to A.A., but I thought it was for sickos like her.

The beginning of my bottom started when I moved out of the house. I was irresponsible and immediately had problems paying my bills on time and staying in college. I did what any good alcoholic would do; I found people to enable me, and I dropped out of college. We all know the rest of the story. I went from job to job in the gay scene. I partied every night at places like Backstreet, Bulldogs, The Armory and Numbers. (Sound familiar?) Blackouts started and recurred with increasing frequency. I slept with three-fourths of the city, and half of the time I would wake up and peek over to see what beauty or beast I was with. All along I thought this was what every gay guy did. I never once dreamed I had a problem. I ended up working on Fire Island one season, which I really did enjoy. Soon after this period, I began to be sent home from work because I could not handle myself appropriately. I was a Dr. Jekyl/ Mr. Hyde drunk. One day, happy; the next day, in a rage. Eventually I was fired from a job as a bartender and rent was due. My roommate threw me out. I don't know what prompted me, but I decided I was ready to do something. I went to a pay phone and called my parents. They said I could come and stay with them only if I were ready to go to A.A. They told me that if I were going to fool around and not be serious, not to come home. You see, the booze and drugs had quit working for me. They had long before this day, but I think my higher power was working in my life, and it was just a coincidence (old timers will tell you there are no coincidences) that I lost my job and my apartment on the same day. I felt like a walking hollow egg. There was nothing left on the inside. I had had enough. I remember looking up into the sky and saying,"God, please help me." He did.

My first question to someone in A.A. was "Can I smoke pot?" I was told that a drug is a drug is a drug. They asked me how I thought I could have a conscious contact with my higher power with a joint in my hand. That made sense, but after about thirty days I did smoke a joint and have a drink. I had to do it one more time; for what reasons I am not sure. That night was the last. It has been almost six years since then, and I can honestly say I am a different person today.

Being the people pleaser that I am, I tried to learn all the slogans and all the right things to say at meetings so everyone would think I was well. It worked, to an extent, but I wasn't growing at all. I went to meetings daily for two years. I went to meetings where mostly straight people went. This was good for me in some ways, but I felt it hard to open up totally. Thank God for the Galano Club in Atlanta. There are several meetings daily there now; when I started there were only two or three meetings per week.

Still, I don't think a gay person with alcohol dependency can use the excuse that because there are not any meetings where mostly gay people go that he can't get sober. Stupid excuses like that are your disease talking to you. It can be done; I did it! An alcoholic is an alcoholic.

I was very scared at meetings at first. I do remember three simple things that I was told to do on a daily basis that I still do. They are: DON'T DRINK AND GO TO A MEETING. ASK YOUR HIGHER POWER TO HELP YOU STAY SOBER EVERY MORNING. SAY THANK YOU TO HIM (OR IT) AT NIGHT.

The beginning of my spiritual awakening began when I realized I was not the only one helping me to stay sober daily. I knew I had never been able to stop on my own, but since I had made a decision to let my Higher Power help, I was getting some time in the program. Things began to work out and to fall into place for the first time ever. I would go to meetings feeling depressed and the topic would be on depression. I carried a lot of guilt from my past with me, and everyone would tell me to do a Fourth Step and Fifth Step to deal with that. Little things like this gave me the faith and courage to go on.

I became very involved in my group and was GSR for two years. Then I began to sponsor people. One day someone told me that of all the people in A.A., he wanted to be just like me! Let me tell you, I almost died. What a feeling of joy mixed with the feeling of if-he-only-really-knew-me! My point is that the sky is the limit once you decide to put both feet into this program.

I am able to be responsible today with my bills. I have excellent credit now. I prayed for a long time, asking God's will for me in a career. The answer came when I enrolled in college five years ago in a Mental Health and Human Services Major. I was terrified that I would not be able to pass my courses and get a degree, but, much to my surprise and joy, I have been on the dean's list 10 times, received numerous academic awards, am in several of the highest honor societies you can be invited into, and next week I will be graduating with honors from Georgia State University. Now isn't that something for an old drunk?

I am presently an addiction therapist at a residential treatment facility in Atlanta. I am very careful to separate my job from my recovery. I cannot substitute my group therapy for my A.A. meetings. Today I take care of myself, too. I eat three meals a day and get eight hours of sleep a night. I try not to get too lonely or too angry either; if I do,

I talk to someone.

I could go on and on about what it's like now. I have gone through some interesting periods. There are times when I don't want to go to meetings, but I know this is when I need them the most. I have not found Mr. Right yet, but I can say that each relationship seems to get better and better.

My life seems to get better and better. I work the program in all areas of my life, and it never lets me down. Honesty is the key to this program and is the thing I have to work the hardest at. I have the most freedom from self and from others that I ever have had; in other words, I love myself enough that I don't have to be in a relationship to feel like a whole person. I do not regret my past. I'm generally happy most days. (I know, I always wanted to vomit when I heard people say this too!)

If one person can relate to my story, then I feel I have accomplished my task. There is hope for us. It is a simple program, not necessarily easy. Hang in there is what I tell myself daily. If I stay around people during the good and the bad, then these times are much easier to get through. If I isolate myself and do not talk about what's going on inside, then I'm headed for trouble.

I am currently thinking of going for a Master's Degree in Social Work and am praying for God's will in my life. If it's meant to be, then it will happen.

17

Coming Out in Sobriety

I am alcoholic and I am gay. These are two facts of my existence today. Growing up, I never expected that being alcoholic and being gay would become basic components of my life. I'm grateful that no one was able to foretell these circumstances earlier in my life. I would not have accepted them as part of my future and probably would have checked out. I'm thirty years old now and have been in the A.A. program for over three years. For the last two years, I've been continuously sober. Sexually, I was a "reluctant" bloomer. I had sex with a man for the first time two years ago. On the whole, my life experience has been a blessing in disguise. Given the opportunity to relive it, there are only a few things about it that I'd change. My past has made me who I am today, and ninety-five percent of the time I like who I am. The best part of my life began several years ago. But it's important to begin my story at the beginning.

I spent my first years as an army brat. My Dad was a gung-ho career soldier and Mom was a house-wife. Dad was my hero; I followed, or tried to follow him, everywhere he went. I don't remember much about my childhood, except that in the second or third grade, Dad had a massive heart attack and was in the hospital for several months. Mom couldn't attend to my Dad in the hospital and take care of my younger brother and me, so I was shipped off to my grandparents' farm in Bentonville, Arkansas. I don't remember much love there; it seems they were concerned about my scholastic ability above all else. I don't remember being held or touched by them in those six or more months I spent with them. A distant cousin, thirteen or fourteen years old, lived nearby, and we were playmates; his parents and my grandparents visited often. In a playhouse out back of my grandparents' house, something happened between him and me. My recollection of what specifically happened has always been vague, but it was something sexual. For twenty-one years, those incidents in the playhouse have often preoccupied my thoughts. I've yearned to understand their full significance.

My father was medically retired from the army at the height of his career and adult life at thirty-seven years of age. A few years later, after his selling cars and then life insurance, we moved from Louisiana to a small farm in Oklahoma. I hated the farm work. I felt like cheap labor, and I could never please my father. My only peace was in the woods, alone, along the river. I went to grade school in nearby Shawnee so I could play football (Dad wanted me to). The school guys and other guys from town intimidated me. I was alone and different, until I turned sixteen and received my driver's license, my first ticket to freedom. I received my driver's license on Thursday , got slightly drunk on Friday night and roaring drunk on Saturday night. Life was great when I was drinking; I was liked and accepted, and finally, for the first time in my life, I was a part of the gang. That summer I bought a truck to haul hay for the local farmers and my Dad. Two friends and I worked all summer long at hauling hay and getting drunk; we loved the freedom. Our parents thought we worked awfully slow, but in reality we worked quickly and drank even faster.

My parents started having marital problems and I began to skip school a lot. The first semester of my junior year of high school, rarely a day went by that I didn't miss at least one class and seldom a week that I didn't miss at least one full day. I was caught the second semester. I had twenty-three absences on record, and my parents weren't aware of twenty-two of them.

I blamed my parents' marital problems on my Dad. I saw everything as his fault. He kept us on a farm in rural Oklahoma, when he'd been successful at selling insurance and cars in the city. He hadn't gotten us out of the city soon enough. Then he ran off, leaving my mother, brother and me on the farm.

I don't remember much about this time of my life. I recall that we moved into a small rented house in Shawnee. Dad soon came back home, but I continued to stay away from the house, drinking nearly every night and getting totally wasted on Friday and Saturday nights. The summer between my junior and senior year was a time that has caused me a great deal of inner turmoil. About midsummer most of my friends went away to Falls Creek, a Southern Baptist youth camp. We made plans for a party the first Saturday night back. I bought a bunch of beer and liquor, and we'd planned to meet at an outdoor dance.

About dark, my friends began to show up, but they wouldn't drink. Every last one of them had been saved. They didn't drink anymore; it was a sin. I was upset, to say the least. I think I drank and got drunk alone that night.

I figured in a few days they'd get back to their normal selves and we'd continue to party. A few weeks went by and they weren't changing back. I finally submitted to their pressure and went to church and to the Fellowship of Christian Athletes meetings. Then it happened, I accepted Jesus Christ as my Lord and Savior and was baptized in the First Baptist Church. There was a sense of God and love I'd never experienced. By the end of the summer I'd been really moved, and, one night, I felt God wanted me to be a minister. I was eventually licensed by the church. Shortly after this, our youth minister left. I was elected by the youth as Youth Council President. The church was without a youth director for about six months, so I more or less took his place. I was in charge of the Wednesday night youth meeting and the Sunday night fellowship. College ministerial students were asked to guide me. I began to prepare and deliver sermons, very evangelistic ones. The college students began to bring their friends. I found that I could make people cry or laugh and experience joy or remorse at my beckoning. The power was wonderful and intoxicating. I was respected and admired; the adults all knew who I was. I'd found my place in life. I was enrolled at Oklahoma Baptist University to become a minister. I re-

ceived grants and scholarships from the local church, from
the university, and through the government. My first year
at college was paid for.

Then a youth minister was hired. He was good and I
didn't feel needed any longer. I was left out and felt useless. I began to drink more. I was graduated from high
school, and my parents moved to Walters, Oklahoma,
about two hours away. I stayed in Shawnee, shared an
apartment with a friend and occasionally worked painting
houses with another friend. One morning I woke up
bored, restless and discontent. I called my uncle, an Army
recruiter, and two weeks later I was in the Army.

I spent four years in the Army. I was a scout in a re-
connaissance platoon in Alaska. I worked with explosives
at Enewetok atoll in the South Pacific and had an administrative position in Ft.Carson, Colorado. I advanced rapidly
in the Army from private to sergeant and received numerous awards and medals, including two Army Commenda-
tion Medals. In three years I learned how to drink in victo-
ry, in defeat and to just pass the time. Staying drunk and
rowdy subdued the sexual urges I was experiencing toward men.

I got out of the Army in June 1980, and came back to
Oklahoma to make my fortune with my Dad in the Oklahoma oil boom. Dad's dreams and plans weren't working
out, so I went to work for Halliburton, an oil field service
company in nearby Duncan. The job was great, little super-
vision and more money than I'd ever seen. In the oil patch,
I learned to drink all day without regard for the time and
to use speed to stay up when needed. The party life was
great, it wasn't unusual for me to spend $300-400 in Law-
ton on my two days off. On what I spent this much, I'll
never know; drinks were only $1.25.

The oil boom busted, and after three years of working
in the oil patch and living the fast life, I was nearly burned
out. I decided to go to school at Central State University in
Edmond, Oklahoma and to use my G.I. bill. I knew my
drinking was a problem, so I controlled it well, for one semester at least. I screwed up the next semester because I

wasn't able to drink all night and then, at the same time, study and go to classes during the day. I dropped out of school and had various jobs including retail sales and delivering keg beer to bars. All I did on that delivery job was drink. I figured it up one time and, on a conservative basis, I was putting away at least forty beers a day. I finally quit delivering draft beers to the bars because the work was interfering with my drinking. The only way I could live like this was to use speed and crank for which I didn't have the money because of my gambling, so I had to steal.

There is a way to charge the bars for beer and not deliver it that made me between $100-$200 a week. In total, I was making about $500 a week and had no bills, except for the rent on my trailer house lot and for utilities which came to less than $200 a month. It was a comfortable living; then I quit my job. I called my boss early one morning, about 7:30 a.m., and asked for the day off. He, of course, said "No," and that I should get myself to work. I bought a six pack and headed to work. By the time I got to the warehouse I had drunk it all, and I told my boss that I'd quit. I'd be damned if anyone was going to tell me what to do. This was the fifth job I'd quit in two years, and it marked the beginning of the end of my drinking career.

In the previous two years, I had distanced myself from my family and was left with only one close friend, though our relationship wasn't healthy because he, too, was a practicing alcoholic. It seemed I was alone and that no one was concerned about me. My drinking accelerated after I quit my job because I had a lot of free time and was depressed.

My close friend's drinking was creating some major difficulties in his life, so his family and girlfriend decided to intervene. I helped them get him into a treatment program for alcohol and drug abuse. With him in treatment, I really was alone. There wasn't anyone I wanted to drink with, and my own drinking was out of control, also. I couldn't get drunk enough to black out, or I'd black out with just a few drinks. My life was miserable and I wanted out. I had fantasies of robbing banks and of either getting away with all the money or getting shot down in the street; either end would have been okay.

I remembered that when I'd taken my friend to treatment, I'd seen A.A. stuff on the walls. It reminded me that there was a chance of help; it reminded me that my grandad had been sober in A.A. for over thirty years.

I called the Oklahoma City A.A. intergroup office one morning. The woman who took the call told me that she'd send some men over to talk with me. I had ambiguous feelings about this, so she made me promise to go to a meeting that night. I drove around the meeting place three or four times before finally deciding to go in. I went in only because of the promise I had made to that woman on the phone.

I have been in A.A. for three and a half years now, and my life has changed more than I could ever have imagined. A.A. has given me the courage to take risks and to experience life. Recovery from alcoholism has been a slow process. One of its hardest challenges is that I have to be honest with myself and others. But the choice was between a miserable existence or the opportunity for a happy and healthy life.

My first thirty days of sobriety were easy. I was on the most wonderful pink cloud, and I felt I'd never need or want to drink again. My pink cloud collapsed when I became obsessed with the thought of doing cocaine. Everything I saw triggered the obsession - Coca Cola machines, PAL Razor blades, small mirrors, and even advertisements for winter skiing with pictures of sparkling snow. My head was throbbing all the time, and I was considering suicide. I was miserable but knew that I'd be more miserable if I drank or used cocaine. I needed help and went to a three-quarter way house for recovering alcoholics and drug addicts. I received a lot of much needed support, understanding and guidance there. I don't think I'd be sober today if that place had not been there to give me a foundation to build on during my eight month stay.

The three-quarter way house taught me to begin to like myself, to trust people, to be responsible, and to be honest and open. But most of all it taught me that I was not alone, I was only alone if I chose to be. Upon my completion of the program at the house, the staff recommended that I make at least three A.A. meetings a week and that I get involved in the A.A. community. I went to meetings and I got involved.

My best friend and I moved into a small two bedroom house. Life was great for us; we both worked part-time and did nothing but hunt, fish and go to A.A. meetings for about five months. I went to A.A. meetings, started a beginner's meeting at a nearby A.A. club, had three sponsorees, spoke monthly at a treatment center, and was the Sunday night speaker at my regular A.A. club. I was Mr. A.A. - respected and admired. But during this five or six month period, I was having terrible periods of depression and cravings to get drunk. I wouldn't admit to myself what was going on with me, and I couldn't talk to anyone because I had this wonderful reputation as Mr. Recovery to uphold; my ego wouldn't allow that reputation to be jeopardized.

My trouble was simple; I wanted to have sex with my roommate. I had never had sex with another man, but it had been a constant desire and fantasy for many years. I felt I was sick and terminally unique. Who could understand, even if I did talk with someone about my homosexual desires? I was going crazy all the time and it finally happened; I got drunk. My drunk started around 2 p.m. and ended around 10 p.m. on Memorial Day. I ended up at an old drinking hangout of mine. I hadn't been back there for one and a half years, but everything and everybody was the same - no change. I did something I had never done before; I left the bar with a half of beer still in the bottle on the table. I had made the decision to get honest with myself and to find someone to help me. I had no choice; it was either to find help or kill myself. I'm grateful that I'd had just enough happiness and serenity in sobriety to know that life could be better

There was one friend who I thought could help me. He was fifty-five years old and had six years of sobriety, and

I'd heard he was gay. I asked him to be my sponsor, and for three weeks I beat around the bush about what had lead me to get drunk after one and a half years of sobriety. Finally, one night, he subtly confronted me about my homosexuality; he had known all along what I had been battling with. We spent many evenings, Saturdays, and Sundays talking about sexuality. Then he told me it was time to do something about it....time to take a chance, to experiment with life to see what I liked or didn't like. Experiment I did. Sex with another man was the most natural thing for me; it was as though I'd been born to it. I was lucky enough to find someone who gently and patiently brought me out with no strings attached. The setting was perfect; the man owned a beautiful house with a sunken tub, a king size canopy bed, and a private pool and garden. For the first time in my life, I felt a part of this world; I belonged here. Coming out of the closet stone sober is an experience I'll always cherish.

In November 1986, I fell head-over-heels in love with a beautiful twenty-year old man, eight years my junior. It was the first time that I felt that another person, other than a family member, really cared about me personally. My sponsor warned me that I was very vulnerable and that the relationship would be over in a couple of weeks. Well, it wasn't - I showed him - this extended trick lasted a full SIX weeks. My young lover left and I was torn apart. My sponsor comforted me as much as possible but never once said, "I told you so." His response was, "Welcome to the wonderful world of relationships."

Up until shortly after my first love experience, I had only been to regular A.A. meetings, so I began going to a gay A.A. group in January. This group gave me love, understanding, compassion and beginner's lessons in the gay, but sober lifestyle. I owe much to the group for the person I am today. I love my life; it is enjoyable and challenging. I can dare to dream today realistic dreams that are becoming reality. My journey to sobriety has matured me. I know that life is to be experienced to its fullest. I also know now that almost everything takes work and time, and that nothing will be handed over on a silver platter, not in business, in relationships, or in sobriety. I've learned that its okay to make mistakes and that I've always got a chance at the good life, as long as I continue not to drink or to use drugs and as long as I continue to go to meetings of Alcoholics Anonymous.

Sobriety has given me the ability to look over a situation, opportunity or experience, regardless of its nature, and to choose to experience it, so long as I've checked out my motives to see if anyone will be harmed (including myself), and so long as I've decided that I'm willing to accept the consequences of my actions. If I don't like the experience, I don't ever have to do it again. Neither guilt or self-pity should come from my actions, as long as I've been honest and open with myself and others about them.

I once heard that in nature there are no rewards or punishments, just consequences. My higher power does not punish or reward me for my actions. What happens to me is the consequences of actions taken by myself and others. What God has given me are the tools to deal with life and its consequences. A.A. helped me find the tools, showed me how to use them, and most importantly taught me that I am not alone.

18

Unending Journey

In Chicago, where I live, there is printed on the back of all the A.A. meeting directories something along the lines of - "I am responsible. Whenever someone, somewhere, reaches out for help, I want the hand of A.A. to be there. And, for that, I am responsible." That means a great deal to me.

The first drink to touch my lips was when I was about thirteen years old. My uncle fooled me into taking a sip of bourbon and 7-Up, telling me it was ginger ale. The result of his joke was that he had to change his shirt, because I spit the foul-tasting stuff on it.

It was about at this time that I noticed that my father had a tendency to have a couple of drinks when he would get home from work, and then go to sleep on the sofa in the living room. I knew he was drinking alcohol, and his behavior distressed me to such an extent that I told my mother that I would never drink, because I didn't want to be an alcoholic like my father.

When I was fifteen, I went to a Christmas party given by my employers for the teenagers at my job. We got to go, unsupervised, out for dinner, and to a play. Our "leader" told us that we were going to get drunk that night. I had no idea what drink to order, but I could remember that Uncle Arthur on "Bewitched" always drank martinis, so I ordered one. By the end of the night, I had had five of them. I don't remember much about that night, except throwing up.

I drank infrequently for the next two years, but every time I started drinking, I did so with the intention of getting drunk. I thought that that was the only reason people drank. I used other drugs, like marijuana, hashish and one time opium, but infrequently because they were more expensive and more of risk legally than alcohol. I was also less partial to drugs than to alcohol because I had had extensive education about drugs in high school, and I was afraid of becoming an addict.

I was graduated from high school a year early and went to a local junior college for two and a half years. Again, I rarely drank or used drugs, although my drug use did increase when I entered college because drugs were more available. In January 1984, I left my parents' home and went to a university in Central Florida. The drinking age in Florida was nineteen; I was also nineteen. It was during the one semester I was at the university in Florida that I started drinking heavily. It seemed as though everyone had a bottle in his room, and I was not opposed to conforming to that custom. I probably drank every night during that semester. I attended the three classes I was registered for, only studied for one of them, and finished the semester with average grades in two classes and an above average grade in the third. I had a part-time job at a delicatessen on campus and spent all of my free time drinking. Either I would drink alone in my dorm room, or I would go out to the bars with one of my girlfriends who knew I was gay.

As the end of the semester grew near, the everyday things in my life began to get unmanagable to such an extent that I told some of my close friends that I thought I was an alcoholic and that, when I got back to Chicago, I was going to start going to A.A. meetings. They told me that I definitely was not an alcoholic. Since that was what I wanted to believe, when I returned to Chicago, I did not go to A.A. Still, I felt as though Florida had turned sour, as far as I was concerned, and that when I got back to my parents, things would be better.

When I got home, I decided that I was not going to return to school. Looking back, I see that going to school got in the way of my drinking. At the time, however, I said that I wanted to work, because I felt that I had gotten little out of going to school.

I thought that returning to my parents' home would make things better; however, I brought my problems (myself) with me. My parents were not pleased that I was drinking heavily in their home, and they were definitely concerned about the large amount of alcohol I was ingesting. I told them to mind their own business and started to make plans to return to Florida where there were people who loved me. In the meantime, I drank and called my friends and ran up phone bills in excess of $200.00 monthly.

It was about this time that I started having frequent disagreements with my father. There was little that we would agree upon. If he told me that the sky was blue, I would say that it was red. I was annoyed at my parents' concern for my welfare as well as angry that I should have to live with such a "dictator" as my father. I would move to Florida as soon as I was financially able, I decided.

One day, my father and I had a major argument. During the course of one shouting match, I threatened to beat him up. He asked me to return to Florida immediately. I left ten days later.

I returned to Florida having neglected several matters, such as like finding a secure place to live with my cat, and remembering that my friends from college were at their respective homes (like Edmonton, Alberta, and Ft. Lauderdale and Syracuse, New York) for summer vacation, and having a job.

At first, I lived in a university dormitory with a woman I had been dating. When she figured out I was using her only for a place to flop, she gave me the boot. Then I started living wherever I could find someone who would let me in the door. I was drinking from the time I awoke, until the time I fell asleep. One night I even spent sleeping in a school bus. I remember that the next day was July 4, 1984. I took myself out to dinner and went to my favorite bar to celebrate the holiday. When I got to the bar, the only money I had left (that is the only form of money I thought of using) was $5.00 in cash.

At the bar on this evening, I met a man whom I started to live with. He advised me that we could use my credit cards to pay for hotel rooms to stay in. Every week or so, I would call my parents to have them send me some cash so that I could pay for anything my boyfriend and I needed that we could not buy with the credit cards. Of course, I never bothered paying the bills on these cards; I just kept using them. Eventually, I surpassed their limits, and we were no longer able to use them.

Both of us started job hunting. The only jobs available that we were qualified for were fast food and construction jobs. My boyfriend chose to use a temporary service that would send him on a different construction site every day. I tried that twice. Being the princess that I was, I didn't take to carrying anything around, much less 20 feet long four-by-fours. I tried to get a couple of jobs for which I was not qualified and failed in these attempts.

I had seen good-looking boys standing on street corners and approaching cars. Sometimes they got into the cars and returned about thirty minutes later, able to purchase anything they needed to get along for a couple of days. After seeing enough of this, I determined that they were hustlers. I had respect for them because, if they could get paid for having sex, they must have been attractive as well as good in bed. I thought that if I could get men to pick me up and pay me for having sex with them, it would mean that I was cute and good in bed, too. So I tried it.

I was successful at it for about three weeks and I probably would have continued hustling but, just before Labor Day, I was arrested for offering to commit prostitution. I spent thirty-six hours in a jail cell with individuals who were very unscrupulous looking. I was scared that if they found out I had been arrested for hustling, they would gang rape me, so I slept the entire time I was there. I was finally seen by a judge and, because I had no police record, he released me on my own recognizance. I was to be in court three weeks later. I never went.

After my release, I went back to my hotel to find a deserted room. My boyfriend had taken everything. I was stunned. I called the desk. They said that they wanted us to move out because they didn't want us ruining the reputation of their establishment. They knew nothing about where my friend had gone. Nearly hysterical, I lay on the bed for about twenty minutes when the phone rang. It was my boyfriend. I told him what had happened to me and asked what had happened to him. He said that when I hadn't come home, he didn't know what had happened, so he called one of his tricks who came and picked him up and took him to his place.

Having no place to live, no money, no clothes except the ones I was wearing, I felt devastated. I called my parents and asked them if I could come home. I did not, and have not to this day, told them about my experience hustling or the fact that I had been jailed. They let me come home.

Things were a little better when I got home. I continued to drink at home and in greater quantities than before. But either my parents were resigned to the fact that they could do nothing about my drinking, or I was less aware of their concern, because, for whatever reason, they seldom hassled me. I returned to the job that I had had since age fifteen and continued where I left off.

During this period, my parents thought that counseling would help. I went to a family counselor who told me that if I could go for a week without drinking, I was not an alcoholic. So for a week I went without drinking. I kept the next appointment to verify it, then went home and resumed drinking with a vengeance. I didn't have much confidence in this counselor because I felt he was a crackpot. We had gone to one appointment together as a family. I had to miss the second appointment because of my work schedule and because of my unwillingness to be flexible about going to see him. When I walked in his office the next time, the first thing he said to me was,"I missed you." My thoughts were — How could you miss me? You don't even know me. I decided that this guy was a joke and told my parents so.

My mother went to another therapist and persuaded me to go see her. I had a few belts before I got there. When I was in her office, we talked about my drinking.

She asked me if I thought I was an alcoholic. I said, "No." She accepted that response, and we spent the rest of the session discussing other areas of my life. I have not seen her since, but I look back on our session and hold a great deal of respect for this woman's abilities.

A month or so passed. I continued to drink, although not as much as I had in Florida. I decided it was time to get a "real" job. I was very fortunate to be hired on the spot by a medical supply company as a data entry clerk. I was thrilled. I believe that I did a good job for them, even though, as time passed, I started drinking more heavily and, on a few occasions, smuggled alcohol into my desk and drank on the job. However, I had a major problem: getting to work on time. This made the company president very annoyed, and we had several meetings on the subject. Finally, one day after I had been there about five months, he gave me an ultimatum: Be in the building and at my desk by 9:00 a.m. If it got to be 9:01 and I wasn't at my desk, he said that I shouldn't bother about coming in at all.

I went home that night and felt very angry. How dare he give me an ultimatum like that! I decided then and there that it was going to be "9:01" for me and that I was not going to return to work for this company. I still had my old job on my part-time basis and would pick up some additional hours there. Without calling, writing them or notifying my superiors in any way, I stopped working for the company. It had gotten in the way of my drinking.

I continued on at my old job, but I started going to work drunk. I would also get drunk and pass out at home and not be able to be awakened to go to work. My mother would call and give different excuses every time this happened. Finally, I was told that my hours had been replaced because I could not be depended upon to be at work.

As my drinking had progressed, my concept of what an alcoholic was had changed. At first, I thought that an alcoholic was someone who drank everyday. When I began to drink everyday, I thought that an alcoholic was someone who drank in the morning. When I drank in the morning, I thought that an alcoholic was someone who lost jobs as a result of drinking. When I lost my job, I admitted I was an alcoholic. The company I have always worked for since I was fifteen (except for the brief period that I was fired and for the time I lived in Florida) is a telephone answering service. One of our clients is the A.A. hotline for one of the local chapters of A.A. As a result of this, I had always been aware of Alcoholics Anonymous and known a little about what the program was like. When I decided that I needed help about my drinking, calling A.A. seemed only logical.

On the day I was fired, I called the man who became my first sponsor. It was April 18, 1985. He told me that I could go to a meeting and gave me directions for getting there. I made the wrong turn and ended up being forty minutes late. Then I got to the building and couldn't figure out where the meeting was being held. In one room were a bunch of people on mats bending and stretching. In the other room was what looked like a P.T.A. meeting. Finally, I asked a groundskeeper which meeting was the A.A. meeting, and he showed me where to go. (I went to the group that looked like a P.T.A. meeting.) I don't remember much about the meeting, except that there was an adorable Italian man there, and I remember saying that I had no self-respect. The group took me out afterward and bought me an ice-cream sundae.

At my first meetings, I heard the things that many newcomers hear: Don't drink, Go to meetings, Do ninety meetings in ninety days, Get a sponsor, Ninety-eight percent of life is just showing up, No major changes in the first year, No relationships in the first year. I went to meetings regularly and learned a great deal.

The first book I was given was *Living Sober*. To this day, this is the first book that I recommend to a newcomer. To me, it is easy to read and explains much of what a newcomer can experience in early sobriety.

I was still having problems dealing with my father's drinking. I talked to my sponsor about it and talked about it at meetings. (I was about five months sober at the time). At one point, my sponsor suggested that if I were in enough pain over the situation, I could always move. It seemed like too big a task to undertake.

Somewhere along the line, I stopped listening to my sponsor and the A.A. group. I started dating a boy who said he also went to meetings. I figured he went to other meetings than the ones I went to because I had never seen him at any, but he seemed to know a lot of the people I knew. Gradually, over a period of two or three months, I went to fewer and fewer meetings, called fewer and fewer people and, eventually, lost touch with the program - all in pursuit of a relationhsip. The result of my wandering from myself and the program and, ultimately, of my stopping attendance at meetings was that I relapsed.

My relapse lasted about sixty days. My new boyfriend relapsed, too. In the past, I had done most of my drinking at home. I sold my father shots for a dollar each to finance my own habit. This time, however, I did most of my drinking at bars. By now, I was of legal drinking age in the state of Illinois, so getting served at bars was not a problem, nor was buying liquor.

In March 1986, after about a month of particularly tumultous existence, my boyfriend broke up with me. I remember the weekend vividly. We had gone out Friday night to our usual nightclub. I had had more martinis than usual - a total of six or seven doubles capped off by a triple. We went home and I passed out cold for the next fourteen hours. When I awakened, he had gone. Sometime during my slumber I was lucid enough to remember his saying that he would come back and pick me up in the evening. I awoke at 8:00, which was just about the time he returned. I was shaking and I was in a cold sweat. I felt very anxious for no apparent reason. I was very apprehensive about leaving my bedroom. I was afraid of continuing to feel the way I was. I told my boyfriend all of this, and he said he had some medicine that would make me feel better. He took me back to his apartment and gave me six or seven pills from various prescription bottles. To this day, I don't know what they were, but they were effective.

He drove me back to my parents' house and said he'd come back in a few hours when the medicine wore off and we would go out. I woke up at midnight, and he was not around. There were four places that I knew he might be at, and I found him at the fourth - back at the bar. I stood behind the barstool he sat on, facing the fish tank and feeling mentally as though everything in the bar were orbiting my head, although I could see that everything was where it belonged. I felt as though I were surrounded by chaos. My boyfriend turned slightly on his barstool and said out of the corner of his mouth to me, "There can never be any kind of relationship between us."

Immediately after he said this, something within me said ---- You don't have to put up with this. You have a choice. You can go back to meetings and this will all change for the better.

We went back to his apartment. I got everything I had ever lent to him, returned to him everything he ever had lent to me, and I went home. I felt so relieved. I arrived at my parents' home at about 5:00 in the morning. My father was awake. I desperately was in need of someone to talk to, so I reached out to my father. I talked to him for two hours, stopping every so often for a short cry. It was one of the few times I have ever cried in front of him since I was older than ten. Then, my mother got up, and I talked to her, almost repeating what I had shared with my father. Then I went to work with my mother (we are employed by the same company). While at work, I shared with a woman friend what had happened to me. After work, I went home, cleaned up and went to my home group's Sunday morning meeting.

After the meeting, I was still in need of someone to talk to. I took many phone numbers and ended up spending the afternoon talking off the ear of an elderly gentleman who was a member of the group and who happened to live a few blocks from me. He also knew my recent boyfriend. I talked with him for three solid hours.

That was March 16, 1986. I was twenty-one years old at the time. I've been going to meetings continuously ever since. That was just a little over two years ago. All of the drinking I have ever done I did over the course of six years prior to that fateful day.

I have come a long way since coming into the program. Admitting and accepting my powerlessness over alcohol was a relief. I had seen the chaos in my life and realized that I could do nothing about it without making some major changes in myself. By coming to meetings, not drinking, having and using a sponsor, and following the advice of the members of my group, I've been able, with the help of my Higher Power, to make some major changes.

When I came back to the program, I was physically very unhealthy, and my appearance was that of someone who has very low self-esteem. My hair was several shades of blond; I looked as though I were pregnant and a few months overdue; my complexion was a mess.

Now my hair is its natural color and is cut in a style that many people have told me is very becoming. I have paid attention to what I eat and how much. I've joined a health club. I'm beginning to look the way I've always known I was capable of looking. In the recent past I've been able to look in the mirror and to be pleased with what I see. This is very new to me and I'm enjoying it. My complexion has cleared up to such an extent that I get many compliments on its quality.

I have moved out of my parents' home and live with two close friends, who are also gay and also recovering. I have grown in my relationship with my parents as well. We see each other infrequently; however, the quality of the time we spend together has improved. I gave a lead at an open meeting and asked them to come. They did, and it meant a great deal to me, although it was quite difficult. I had not been that open with them in the past. I hugged my father for the first time in several years on that day.

I have come to the realization that, for now, I am incapable of handling credit or a bank account and, instead, handle everything with cash. Though I may be short of funds sometimes, I find that I have an almost limitless supply of patience. I have found a Higher Power who carries me through the rough times and attends to me. We share the good times and the bad, and I know that He will not give me anything I cannot handle. Sometimes I feel a lack of faith without realizing it, and my Higher Power finds people to remind me of its constant presence and care. I find myself thanking my Higher Power many times throughout the day for small things as well as big things. I find that the smaller things mean a great deal more to me than they did before, and I feel this is good for me because I find much more continual happiness than I did before.

I no longer have to take responsibility for things I am powerless about. I no longer have to be a doormat for people. I can say what I believe and people do not ridicule me. I respect myself and my ideas, and I find that people seem to respect me as well. I can take care of my physical, emotional and spiritual needs today as I never could before. All of these dramatic changes are due to this program. The longer I am in the program, the more I am aware that the journey I have started is unending. The more I learn, the more I see how much I have to learn. When I remember these things and am in the right frame of mind (which happens more and more frequently), I feel a great deal of gratitude to my Higher Power that I have been chosen to take this journey.

I feel that doing service work has played a major role in my recovery. Beginning at about six months of sobriety, I have almost continually been chairing one meeting or another. I grow a lot as a result of chairing meetings. In addition, I have also worked on committees for fund-raising for various groups, including for Chicago's annual round-up. I feel so much gratitude when I see the results of my efforts that the effort required seems trite. Recently, I was trained as and am now a volunteer on the local gay hotline. The hotline offers referrals to community agencies, and information on bars as well as on counseling services. This also brings me good feelings.

Another good area of service, that is new to me, is working with newcomers. I currently sponsor two men whom I am proud to know. They are a great benefit to my own recovery, and they have expressed similar feelings about me. There is little that gives me as great a feeling of gratitude as does working with a newcomer.

For me, sex and relationships in recovery have been ongoing concerns. Having sex while sober has never been a problem. However, there are many aspects to relationships (including ones containing sex) that are new and foreign to me. In the past, I never had enough self-esteem to practice safe sex. Now I do. My attitude in the past was, if someone was a great lay, he was someone I might be interested in starting a relationship with. My attitude and behavior in this area are starting to change. I met a nice man recently and, instead of taking him home and throwing him on his back, we exchanged phone numbers and are going on a date! As I said, this is new, so it is a little weird, but I think it's an approach worth trying.

And so my recovery continues.....Today. For that, I am responsible.

19

Seed of Hope

I came down the chute in April of 1965 to face a world that I was not destined to be able to cope with until years later. I consider my recovery to be a rediscovery of a potential that I had, but due to a disease, was unable to utilize.

I arrived as the second child. Eleven months later, my birth was followed by that of my younger sister. My older sister grew into the hero of the children, and I idolized her and envied her successes. My younger sister gained success from tears and sweat wrought from determination. I was lost from the start. I couldn't discover the discipline to gain the quiet success of my older sister, and I didn't have the passion about school like my younger sister to cause the attitude of "I'll keep at it until I get it right."

I was not popular. I had an adequate amount of friends (mostly girls) that kept the teachers content to know that I was not a loner and was not destined to be a football star. In the fourth grade, when we chose names for the Christmas gift exchange, I drew my own name. Too afraid of the reaction that would be caused by telling the class that someone would have to put their name back and get mine, I kept the secret. I bought myself a toy and simply kept quiet about who had given it to me. No one questioned me. I felt alone and safe. When teams were being chosen for sports, I died a thousand deaths feeling that I would be a burden to whatever team was unfortunate enough to get the last pick, me.

I found escape in the form of extra-curricular activities. I loved the sensation of an audience applauding. Natural musical and dramatic talent helped. This form of escape followed me through my active addiction which started in high school.

Going from a private grade school and junior high to a public high school with some rather rough-types was disarming to my security system. My friends were getting high, and I decided to ease the pain. Alcohol was my first drug. Twelve mixed drinks followed by three shots of tequila did the trick. I was born with a tolerance. Because I hated high school, I decided to escape to college and thus dropped out and became a college freshman.

Art education was my major. I felt that it was respectable to try to expand my mind with ritualistic use of hallucinogens. Drinking became a favorite pastime. After reviewing my portfolio, one professor asked me if I were on drugs. I flatly denied his accusations. My grades were dropping and my interest in art was more in hallucinations than in reality.

The addiction became a road map to sexual experiences. I was aware of my sexuality since about the age of six when I realized that I wanted to be the son of a magician on a local TV show. (He was that cute.) In retrospect, my addiction was evident by about that age as well. I remember Art Linkletter asking a panel of children who they would want for their parents if they could chose. I wanted Liz Taylor and Richard Burton. Surprise.

On the night of my 18th birthday, I sat with a friend in a drunken stupor and overheard a group of men at the next table talking about having been to a gay meeting. I leaned over toward them and, in my most humble way, offered up my inebriated virginity. One seemingly gentle soul took me up on my quest for emancipation and took to me his apartment where he proceeded to rape me. I interpreted this as how men treated each other in the gay world, and I believed that this was what intimacy between adults was all about. This form of intimacy took me to public toilets, rest stops and bathhouses where I tried to find Prince Charming by letting almost any man have whatever he wanted. I changed colleges, changed majors, and moved to different states trying to find comfort. Years later, I discovered that I had been running away from the source of comfort, my higher power.

Becoming an A Queen in Terre Haute, Indiana is not really a difficult task if you still have a pulse and are not attached to a respirator. I was the belle of the bar. I would trick, drink, trick again, and then go home alone. I graduated with a respectable grade point average and a degree in nursing. In my senior year, the third woman I had sex with became pregnant, so we got married. We remained married for eight years producing two wonderful children. I was a living mess of lies, frustration, anger, resentments, confusion, and addiction. I had no method of saying no. If shame were implied or overtly spoken, I would try to do what was expected.

I found myself teaching public speaking to 90 students, being a full-time graduate student, and working full-time night shifts in an intensive care unit trying to make those around me happy. I realized that I wanted out and had no clue of where the door was located. I attempted suicide by injecting a drug meant to paralyze. I became weak enough that I couldn't inject any more of the drug and yet was still breathing. I developed a pattern after that of coming home from work and drinking milkshakes made with half a fifth of whiskey or sherry, injecting some pain killer, and then calling hospitals all over the country collect that were advertising for nurses. Unaware of the concept of geographical cure seeking, I moved and moved toward my bottom.

I was back in management at a hospital that I had worked in before. I had changed and attributed all the changes to anything and anyone else. I spent five to six nights at the gay bars in a perpetual state of misery and aloneness. I knew that if I could just find Mr. Right, all would be well. My boss called me one morning and said she wanted to see me. I entered her office and saw the documentation of my drug use on her desk. "You are an addict," she said. "Yes," I stated for the first time ever. I felt a relief like I had never felt in my life. I didn't know what was about to happen, but I knew it couldn't be worse than what I had been living.

I was sent to treatment and returned to the serenity of meetings, sponsorship, and recovery. I lost my license to practice nursing, so I was demoted and suffered a decreased salary. After being demoted a second time, I became a secretary working in an office where I had been associated with in the past as management. I kept repeating to myself that God was trying to teach me about humility and pride. Something worked. I stuck it out and finally had my nursing license returned. The next day, I was given the keys to the entire institution, including those to the pharmacy, because of the trust I had earned. Due to the support and growth I have gotten from the 12 step fellowships, I have been able to be drug and alcohol free ever since.

Early in recovery, my fears were getting the best of me, and my sponsor taught me to take each problem/situation/fear through the steps. The freedom that this process gave me was my first spiritual awakening. Coming to terms with my sexuality in a healthy fashion, I have worked through the steps several times. I have come to understand my recovery, my sexuality and my life as gifts that need to be celebrated. Somehow, a seed of hope was planted years ago before I found the 12 steps. That hope is now a tree that when I am afraid, I can crawl up into and look at the world feeling protected and safe. Today I am grateful for all of the gay men and others in A.A. I say thank you for all being there when I need you, and thank you for loving me when I tried to convince you that I am unlovable. I am not the human slug I once assumed I was. I am a creation full of the love of recovery. If it works for me, it can work for any gay recovering alcoholic man.

20

Freedom in the Big Sky Country

Every person has to deal with his own unique set of life circumstances with which he must struggle. Typically, these circumstances aren't fair. But fairness is not an issue; reality is what we have to deal with.

I am a gay 42-year-old recovering alcoholic and am finally coming to terms with reality. It has been a long struggle, and the struggle is not over until my soul leaves my body at my death.

As I think is the case with most alcoholics, I drank alcoholically the first time I ever had a drink. I drank fast, and I drank strong drinks. I threw up, passed out, and didn't remember a lot of what happened. I had horrendous hangovers, and I LOVED IT! Something had always seemed to be missing in my life up until the time I began drinking; that missing something was alcohol.

The first time I drank I was dating a girl. I didn't really have a romantic interest in her, because I knew that I was turned on by guys. But she was a good cover and a convenient crutch to support and validate my masculinity. I believe my parents knew that I had gay tendencies from the time I was a small child, and they did all they could to discourage such behavior. My father, especially, talked as badly about "queers" as he possibly could, and my mother would over-react any time she thought that I might be thinking "that way." And these were intelligent people - my father had a degree in both law and medicine. So I grew up believing that to be queer was bad, that queer thoughts were bad, and that queers had no place in our society. The message was clear: I could not be who I wanted to be. I felt coerced to pass as straight. In the process of passing, however, I used and abused my friendship with my "girlfriend," continually behaved in ways that were not true to myself and, basically, presented a false image of who I was - and all to make sure that everyone was happy with the person I was.... everyone, that is, except for me.

I was still in high school when I had that first drink. Alcohol made me feel good about myself, and I really could fit into the world when I was intoxicated. It was to be my friend for the next twenty-two years - at least I thought it was my friend.

My father died when I was sixteen. I was glad. He and I had never gotten along well. He was always trying to make a MAN out of me, and we always had to do these macho things - hauling rocks, fixing motors, constructing things; I hated every minute of being with my father. If I made a mistake, I was severely reprimanded for it. One time, when we were building a fence, I broke a drill bit. My father knocked me down on the ground and started kicking me and just couldn't seem to stop. My mother heard me screaming and called the sheriff. That was one time when I truly thought I would die. And, of course, all the time he was kicking me, he was calling me every derogatory name for a gay person that he could think of. My life with my father was a nightmare. I don't remember that he ever expressed or indicated any love for me. My impression is that he was sorry that I'd been born and that he wished me dead. Not surprisingly, I felt no love for him. I felt more than relief when he died; I felt truly happy. But it wasn't until I sobered up that I could stop feeling guilty for having felt happy about his death.

My first year of college was at an all-men's private college in Menlo Park, California. One day my roommate and I started talking about our likes and dislikes, and he soon figured out that I was one of "those." He spent the night in the bathroom, even though I hadn't made any advances toward him (I never have been the aggressor). The next day he reported me to the Dean of Men, who, in turn, sent me to a psychiatrist to help determine whether I was "normal." Of course, by this time I had learned to give all the right answers, and I was still hanging on to my old girlfriend, so I passed the inquisition. To make sure that nothing happened, however, I was assigned a single room, and I kept my place for the rest of the year.

I transferred to Montana State University in Bozeman, where I spent the next three years and from where I was graduated. I got a degree in accounting, much to my mother's dismay, because she had heard that a lot of "faggots" become accountants. Of course, she let me know of her displeasure. As for my girlfriend, she had gotten tired of waiting and married someone else. I put on the sad act, but was really relieved that I had gotten out of that relationship. I had never had a sexual interest in females and had always used the excuse that I was practicing being a good Christian when the subject of having intercourse came up. Actually, I had become heavily involved in church work and, indeed, did think that I was a spiritual person.

My drinking increased throughout my college years, and my reluctance to be chummy with roommates continued. I was always afraid that demonstrations of affection would invariably be interpreted as sexual come-ons. I was afraid that I would be kicked out of school for homosexual behavior, and I couldn't dishonor my family in that way.

Right after college I was drafted into the Army (this was during the Vietnam conflict). I was stationed in Germany and found, if I acted drunk enough, that I could get away with making advances toward another guy. The only time I tried it was on a train going to West Berlin, and I loved it! The only times I had sex with men before was with some Catholic priests. I knew that having sex with a man was bad, and they were men of God, so I was very confused about the matter, but I couldn't talk it over with anyone.

I became a bank examiner after my tour of duty in the Army, and my drinking really blossomed. Drinking was encouraged in banking circles, and, of course, everyone expected the traveling man to drink. I worked with three other men, one of whom I really had a crush on. I think that he knew it, and he always let me know what he thought of homosexuals (he was not tolerant). We usually had single rooms, but on one occasion my heart-throb, Bob, and I had to share a room. We had a few snorts, and then Bob went to take a shower. I was also going to go into the bathroom while he was in the shower, under the pretense that I had to take a leak. When I tried the door-knob, it was locked! I was mad and humiliated, because I knew that he had figured me out

The other examiner turned out to be an alcoholic also, and I would undress him when he passed out. Of course, I was never in much better condition than he was, so it wasn't a hell of a lot of fun. Although sometimes I think he knew that I was undressing him, he never said any-thing to me about it when we were sober. If he had, I, of course, could always have used the pretext that I was so drunk that I didn't know what I had been doing.

I really didn't have many sexual experiences during my drinking years, because I always felt intense guilt after having sex with another man. I believed that it was bad and that I was bad.

In 1984, I lost my job with the bank in Butte, Montana. I was on unemployment for six months and thought that I was in heaven. I was financially secure and drank a case of Black Velvet every week and a half. I explained to the woman clerk at the liquor store that I was buying the booze for four little old ladies, who were undoubtedly al-coholic, and that they all played cards together every day. The liquor store clerk couldn't have cared less, but I felt compelled to cover myself one more time.

I knew that my drinking was getting out of hand. I hated what I was doing, but I was powerless to stop. I be-came extremely paranoid; the telephone ringing would send me to a corner of the living room where I would cry because I was so afraid of it. I was a maintenance drinker; I never went on binges; instead, I drank every day. Before I started my day's drinking, I would put supper in the re-frigerator in a certain spot. The next morning when I got up, I would check to see if the supper was still there. If it wasn't, I knew that I had eaten the night before. Almost from the first drink, I blacked out everything throughout the night. Sometimes I called people on the telephone, and, oddly enough, they seldom realized that I was drunk. I had learned how to talk normally and even how to act normally, no matter how much I had had to drink. I never was one of those drunks who just lets everything hang out and has a hell of a good time. I always was trying to act respectable. When people would talk to me a few days later about conversations we had had while I was drunk, I was always amazed at some of the things I had told them. I knew I had a very active imagination, but, of course, I never remembered what I had said. I always encouraged them (sometimes to my amusement, sometimes to my chagrin) to relate the stories that I told at times.

I knew that my drinking was getting out of hand, but I also knew that I was bad because I was gay, and I didn't know which was worse. When we were children, we used to play the game which went something like this: How would you rather die - would you rather be slowly skinned alive or be tied to a red ant hill and have the ants eat you alive? I was pretty much in the same position: Which was the worse circumstance - being gay or being alcoholic? I was receiving the gay newsletter called "Out in Montana" at the time, and there was an article in one of the issues written by an alcoholic lesbian. The article mentioned that a gay A.A. group was in Missoula, so I thought that I could get a handle on both problems at the same time, if I could participate in such a group. I phoned the contact person for the gay A.A. group, who informed me that there was no gay A.A. in Butte (after all, this is a mining man's town), but that my first priority was to get sober, regardless of my sexual orientation. I will be forever grateful to him for setting my priorities straight - I thought that my primary problem was that I was gay.

I attended my first meeting of Alcoholics Anonymous on December 16, 1984, and have been sober since that time. I refused to go to treatment because of my mistaken notion that in treatment you were tied down in a bed in a barracks-like room with everyone around going through

D.T.'s. I now know differently and, indeed, would have opted for such treatment. But I also know that a person can learn to live sober without having the benefit of a treatment center.

After I sobered up, I told my sponsor that I was gay. It was extremely painful for me to tell him, because I didn't know if he would continue to be my sponsor after my confession. But he is a very understanding Native American and, while he didn't understand too much about being gay, he was willing to help me work through this problem. I love that man today with all my heart for trying to understand me and for working with me. He is still my sponsor and is truly one of the most wonderful people I have met. When I told him my awful secret, we were sitting in his pickup. I was awash in my tears. All he did was listen, and I tore my guts up telling him what I'd never put into words before. Hours later, when I had said all that there was to tell, I got out of his pickup and walked toward my own car. During those minutes, I was the loneliest person on earth. My sponsor started to drive off, slowed down, stopped, then turned around and came back. He got out of his pickup, walked over to me and gave me a hug. That was the most important embrace I have ever received in my life. To this day, I still become very emotional just thinking about that moment.

A couple of years later, I went to an A.A. meeting at which a young Marine from a base in North Carolina was a guest. He was in great anguish because his sponsor, who was also in the Marines, had told him that he was gay. This young man really liked his sponsor but was not sure how to respond to this new development.

I had never heard this kind of a problem brought up at a meeting before. All of a sudden my heart started pounding in my ears, my face was burning, and I started sweating. Several people had to talk before it was my turn, and I frantically debated with myself whether I should address his concern. I was conditioned to assume some risk existed for me by my coming out to the group. On the other hand, the opportunity to ease this Marine's fears, by relating how I could empathize personally with the sponsor, seemed very considerable. I decided to take the risk of rejection by my A.A. group and to go for it.

When it became my turn to talk, I told this young man that his sponsor probably didn't want to be gay any more than he wanted to be an alcoholic. I stated that I understood his sponsor's situation because, like him, I, too, was both alcoholic and gay. Dead silence swept across the room. I continued by explaining that, when I hugged people after the meeting, the guys shouldn't think anything of it - that my hugs were only gestures of friendliness. After the meeting, EVERYONE at the meeting hugged me, and that young Marine was the first in line.

Now that I am out of the closet, I find a new freedom. Just as I had freedom from alcohol when I sobered up; I have a freedom from that awful secret once I brought it out of its closet. It has not been easy. Two of my sisters always knew that I was gay, but the third one doesn't want anything to do with me because of my homosexuality. But that is her problem, not mine; that's the way I look at the situation now. Every single person in the community of Alcoholics Anonymous, however, has accepted me for who I am. I love A.A.; within this association are the most tolerant and loving people on earth. They may not agree with my "preference," but they still accept me.

With regard to my homosexuality, never have I felt that I ever had a choice. I have never had heterosexual erotic feelings or fantasies. If I had had a choice, do you think that I would ever have opted for a gay lifestyle? Hell, no! After all, I am an alcoholic, and I want things to be as easy as possible for me. While I don't go around advertising that I am gay, I did tell one of my neighbors, who brought me some material written by a gay recovering alcoholic friend of his. This material has opened up a world of understanding that I didn't even know existed. I had a young man living with me who was heterosexual, though he knew that I was gay. While we never had sex, I became infatuated with him and fell in love for the first time in my life. He had less than a year of sobriety when he started drinking again and moved out. The effect has been devastating for me. It is not easy to go through an experience at forty-two that most people have in their late teens and early twenties. I am not as resilient as those younger people. But now I do know what infatuation is like, and I know what it is like to lose one's first love. These vital experiences of life I would never have had were I still drinking.

Life isn't always fair, but we can learn to live with the reality of our changing situations in life. Today I have hope in my heart and a future to look forward to. I don't want merely to exist until I die; I want to LIVE until death claims me. I can only do that sober. And now that I have released myself from those awful shackles of the secrecy of being gay, I feel that I'm as ready as I ever shall be to live as the person I was meant to be.

21

Don't Delay - I Did

I am gay and a white Anglo-Saxon Protestant. March 12 is my birthday; Pisces, my sign. My parents were non-drinkers. They were also church-goers, but not fanatical about it. My mother was warm and emotional; my father, quiet and reserved.

When I was thirteen, I had my first drink - homemade chokecherry wine at the house of a school friend. It made me ill, and that was it - no buzz.

During the last couple of years of high school, several friends and I would reserve Friday evenings for drinking beer at the tavern which catered to students from the local university. In order to justify each occasion (Do I hear "rationalization" from anybody?), we would look in the local newspaper to see what famous person was having a birthday that day. A birthday celebration was our excuse for drinking for two or three hours and getting a little drunk. We were convinced that we were quite sophisticated young men.

Despite some "plain sewing" (mutual masturbation) with my cousin and a couple of school friends, my thoughts and desires were heterosexual. I was going out occasionally with one girl who would not let me go beyond clitoral manipulation. But another girl I dated invited me for a weekend to her home in the country. I seduced her in the front seat of her mother's car. (Her mother was not along for the ride.) Thus, I lost my virginity, but I was not impressed by the experience. I started running around with a third girl to dances and private parties where there was always quite a bit of drinking, but no sex.

I finished high school and began college, but World War II intervened. I joined the Navy. Because I wore glasses, I was assigned to be a radio operator. I was in the Navy for five years, three of which were spent at sea. Halfway through my tour of duty, I was commissioned an officer. Impressed by my own abilities and flushed with elation, I proposed to and married the third girl - the one I'd been running around with - the party girl.

During my stint in the navy, because of much intensive training and much time out at sea, my drinking had been slowly increasing, though it always seemed about normal to me at the time. I did get drunk quite a few times, however. I had one friend on board ship who had my rank and was from my home town. Sometimes, when I was drunk, we had sex - nothing lovey-dovey, just sex. On all of those occasions, I was the aggressor. I still remember his name and remember that I was attracted to him.

At the end of the war, I declined to stay in the navy. Upon my honorable discharge and leave, I collected my wife and moved to a job in, what was for me, a very small town of 22,000 inhabitants. My wife became pregnant - unplanned and unwanted, but abortion was not even considered. In my immaturity, I was unhappy and resentful of the marriage, of the pregnancy, of my job and of being without anyone to counsel or to guide me. My drinking increased greatly. Most evenings I spent drinking, and the more I drank, the more I neglected my wife. Finally, I asked for a divorce. My wife agreed. She refused to accept alimony, so I was only responsible for child support payments. She went home to mother, taking our baby daughter with her. I quit my job and moved to the west coast.

For the next six years, my drinking got worse. I also came out into the gay world as a self-acknowledged homosexual shortly after the divorce. After an initial period of great promiscuity, I settled down with one man. He and I bought a house where we lived with his mother and an elderly, retired family friend. As my drinking got worse, I began cheating on my lover, until I left him for another man.

I made a move to the east coast; then another back to the west coast to rejoin my second lover in San Francisco. All the time my drinking kept increasing, but my lover did not complain or criticize me because (as I realized years later) my drinking made it very easy for him to manipulate me. We had a couple of separations (I was always the one who walked out), but I always returned.

In 1965, during one of these temporary "divorces," I found myself living alone. I had alienated my few friends because I was always drunk when they saw me, and I behaved like a fool. My drinking pattern was to stop work at 4:30 p.m., make for my favorite gay bar (a neighborhood-type place), and drink highballs (usually vodka and soda) for two hours or so. Then I'd go home, have a bite to eat, proceed to sit in front of the T.V. and drink until a stupor set in and I was just able to get into bed. The pattern never varied; it was automatic.

One Friday evening I got a crying jag, which was rare, but I was desperately lonely. I left my apartment and went to a local church for some reason. I could not get in, so I went home and, as usual, drank myself into oblivion. However, that evening was my bottom. The next morning, a Saturday, I phoned A.A.

The lady at the San Francisco A.A. Central Office was absolutely wonderful. Despite my being as difficult as possible, she hung in there and finally obtained from me a commitment to go to a meeting the coming Monday. I had my last drink on the Sunday before. At 7:55 p.m. on Monday, December 6, 1965, I entered a church basement to attend my first A.A. meeting. I have not had a drink since.

During my formative early years in A.A., several things stand out that are of great importance to me. Initially, I was very suspicious of A.A. people who helped me, wondering what it would cost me. I finally awoke to the fact that there were no strings attached. I had great difficulty in surrendering, continuing to think that "I can handle it" for everything. It was pointed out to me, with elementary logic, that if that were so, why had I found it necessary to come to A.A.? Well, I had no answer. And, as I have heard from many other people in A.A., living one day at a time was well nigh impossible at first, because I persisted in living in the past and carrying guilt on one shoulder and remorse on the other. It took awhile before I was able to overcome doing this.

After joining A.A., I moved back in with my former lover, but this time as companions. After many years of living together, we separated. I now live alone, as does he.

I have been very active in A.A. for a long, long time, have occupied the various offices of groups and have attended meetings with great regularity.

At present, I attend from two to five meetings a week and go to at least one gay out-of-town A.A. convention per year. I'm on the list for both gay and straight 12-Step calls through our local suburban central office, and I sponsor several people, gay and straight, male and female. Locally, I am regarded as some sort of a pioneer, as an advisor and as an upholder of tradition-by-the-Big-Book. I think I'm thought of as being tough as a sponsor and a little stand-offish as a person (which is a characteristic I'm trying to overcome).

I think that, emotionally, I'm a fairly stable individual. Physically, I'm very active and in excellent condition. My sex drive is strong, but I'm not as young and handsome as I used to be, and I don't wish to be promiscuous, though I'm always on the look out for someone I can care about and look after. As I grow older, the specter of living alone looms large, but I resolutely turn it over to my Higher Power. The great sustaining conviction I carry in my life is that when I have a problem and do my level best to solve it, but get nowhere, I can say, "Lord, I need your help," and I get it. I owe A.A. everything, because through it I was able to choose sobriety. And sobriety is the number one priority in my life, taking precedence over everything else.

22

Gay, Sober, and Grateful

I am a thirty-seven year old real estate broker. I live in Chicago, where I was born and raised in an upper-middle class family. I am also homosexual and a recovering alcoholic with 54 weeks of sobriety. The single word that captures the way I feel today is: gratitude. In fact, sometimes I am overwhelmed with gratitude for the wonderful changes that have taken place in my life during the last year. I realize now that most of the problems in my life before sobriety were caused by me. I take responsibility for those traumas, and I am extremely happy I have the choice today of not allowing them to recur.

In the spring of 1986, I wanted to kill myself. I thought I had nothing left to live for. I had no serious friends. The only people I hung around with were practicing alcoholics like me. We cried and complained together about how terrible life was for us. Basically, my friends and I thought we were worthless individuals. Little did we know we were making our own lives miserable.

I was consumed by self-pity about my past life. I tortured myself with memories of all the terrible things that had happened to me. I constantly suffered from a perpetual case of herpes that covered much of my body. The open sores kept me from having regular sex because I knew better and had enough decency than to infect other people. In a word, I felt miserable. But, today, my herpes sores are dried up. Only scars of that infection remain, but I know when I am getting upset because I can feel the old lesions begin to throb. I instantly calm down. They remind me of the A.A. expression: "Easy does it."

My parents are still practicing alcoholics. They used to serve me and my two older brothers wine at the dinner table from the time I was six, but I did not drink alcoholically until I was sixteen. In high school I made a friend whose father was a practicing alcoholic. Through him we had an endless supply of beer for our weekend binges. But I am getting ahead of myself.

Although I was never physically abused as a child, I was abused emotionally by my parents. This abuse led to deep and bitter anger and resentments not only toward my parents, but also towards my nurse. In fact it wasn't until I received therapy in adulthood that I could begin trusting females.

My life at elementary school started as a means of escaping my abusive home life, but very quickly I learned to dread being there, as well. My classmates criticized me and teased me endlessly because of the terrible time I had reading and writing and playing any kind of sports activity. I was always the last person selected for teams, and the captain of my team always protested loudly when he saw I was about to join his group. My self-esteem was nil.

At age 17, I had a routine eye examination which disclosed that I was dyslexic. The doctor's explanation washed away all the fears and self-hatred I had had about my inability to read, to write, and to coordinate my eye and hand movements on the playing field. I immediately forgave my classmates for hating my lack of coordination, but I could not forgive the endless number of teachers and psychologists who tested my I.Q. every few months. The results were always the same; I was an intelligent person who could not read or write well. I must be "lazy," was the diagnosis. I took these "experts'" words as conclusive evidence of my lack of personal worth.

Once I knew why I could not read, I decided I would ignore the people who had hurt me so badly. Very slowly and deliberately, I taught myself how to read and write. It took me weeks, but the struggle was well worth the effort. Today, I love to write as a hobby, and I used to be one of the lay readers at my former church; only the minister knew I was dyslexic. I could read as well as anyone there who had normal vision and normal reading ability.

By the time I was 17 and had worked out of my dyslexic condition, I had been drinking alcoholically for a year. I secretly loved to indulge in my drinking and, then, to revel over my self-directed recovery. I was rapidly casting out the rest of the world because I thought I could fix, charge and direct myself. I was also scared someone would criticize me for being who I was. I couldn't handle any form of criticism.

By the time I was 20, I had had enough of being the referee for the battles of my alcoholic parents. I left home, never to live there again.

I had left home once before when I was 13, though under different circumstances and only for two years. My two older brothers were attending east coast boarding schools at the time, and I convinced my parents that I needed to join them. It was my way of escaping my hateful and hated classmates and my parents (whom I now detested).

My first homosexual experiences occurred during those two years away from Chicago. The boy with whom I was sexually active was caught in a compromising position with another boy in the school infirmary. Both young men were expelled from school that day. I was crushed with guilt and remorse when the headmaster quoted from the book of Leviticus that homosexuality is an "abomination" in the sight of the Lord. I was certain God hated me as much as I hated myself. I dove into the closet and stayed there sexually and emotionally, for the next twenty years.

I was convinced I was a sinner who was eternally damned to hell. Only when I was thirty-three, and deeply in love with a gay Presbyterian minister, did I discover that I had not violated the tenets of Leviticus. Before this relationship, I had never made love to another man; I had only had sex. "I'm saved!", I thought. Ever since that first love-making experience, I have been glad to be homosexual. I did not fully appreciate my radically changed attitude and it didn't have much of a chance to mature, however, until I experienced gay meetings of Alcoholics Anonymous. In the last year, I have learned that God made me homosexual. My sexual identity and orientation is a gift from a loving deity, not a curse. I truly believe that God loves me, and that He made me in His image, which is, in part, gay.

Before I joined A.A., however, I was not convinced I was a good person, or a moral one, so I clung socially to other gay men who were clergymen. I figured that if I were going to hell, so were they, and I would be in good company! Today, I do not care what my friends do for a living. I have one friend who is an Episcopal priest, but I do not like him because of his profession. I simply think the man is a nice person.

My life stumbled along after I left home. I entered the real estate business in order to imitate my father. I thought maybe, then, he would approve of me, but he never did. However, I grew to love the business and I have remained in sales and management for the last sixteen years. I spent one short year as a clerk in a bank before returning to the job I love.

I began my adult life encumbered with two damaging childhood messages that I had internalized: my body was sinful, and so was sex. My nurse had given me these messages when I was maybe five or six. They plagued me constantly. I drank alcoholically to hide the pain they caused me, because I believed they were true. I have always trusted people I love, and I have tended to carry their messages wherever I go. This characteristic about me has hurt me often, but it has also made me a very fast learner in the program of A.A.

To escape from the self-loathing these messages evoked, I would drink heavily, often at one of the local gay bars where male strippers danced every night. I became close friends with many of the performers. One of them trusted me enough to hold his straw hat over his genitals when he danced. My alcoholic ego absolutely loved the attention! I grew to love my own body through experiencing the joy of other people's physiques. Gradually, I was able to address the other major cause of fear and self-loathing in my life: sex.

I was feeling lonely and alone. It was 1980. Twenty of my twenty-nine closest friends and relatives died during that year. I was nearly crazy from feeling abandoned. Compulsively, I went to the local gay pornographic theater where I threw my body at whoever would have me. Generally, my sex partners were lonely, less attractive older men. To quote a once popular song: "I was looking for love (and validation) in all the wrong places." I wanted other people to love and to validate my existence, because I did not love myself or think that my life was worth living. But every night I left the theater feeling lonelier and more emotionally empty than when I had entered the place. I must have been insane. I thought that by returning to the theater every night, I would find the man of my dreams who would make me feel good about myself. Little did I know that feeling good about myself first had to come from within before someone else could share those feelings about me from without. I was half a person, looking for another half a person, in order to make a whole, complete individual. My search was never successful; indeed, it never could have been.

I only left the theater when one of my sex partners tried to strangle me in the booth we were in. I grabbed my clothes and shoes and ran naked from the stall. Shouts of "Go, girl, go!" greeted me as I ran in terror for my life to a nearby stall where I got dressed before I went home.

The next night, I was at my favorite bar, looking for sex partners in what I thought would be a "safer" place. It wasn't. The man I picked up, I thought I could trust. I took him home. We had some very unsatisfying sex, after which I fell sound asleep. The combination of the booze and the sex always knocked me out. I awoke the next morning to find that my guest had left sometime during the night. I also discovered that he'd taken with him my full length man's mink coat and five designer suits valued at $500 each. I felt emotionally raped and furious at myself. Up until that point, I had never discussed my homosexuality with anyone, but I called the police and made sure the officer knew the theft was homosexually related. I was terrified to talk about myself in this way, but it hurt too much for me to keep silent any longer. I then called the insurance company. I was referred to the claims department where I talked to an absolutely wonderful woman. She listened with complete professionalism to my story and then suggested in her best Yiddish grandmother's accent, that, next time, I go to his place! Through my tears of anguish, I was able to roar with laughter.

I resolved at that moment that I was going to slow down sexually, but it was Halloween weekend 1982. Immediately, I went out and found myself a "lover." It was the Presbyterian minister. We were together for four months; then I threw the man out. I did the same thing to eleven other men over the next three and a half years. I became blase´ about my ability to attract men and, then, to dump them. I even dubbed myself the "Elizabeth Taylor" of the gay community, so as to fend off any potential criticism from my friends, but I continued to drink alcoholically because of the number of men I was running through and running over in my life. Today, however, I appreciate the quality of other men. I view them with respect and love, which reflects the same newly found feelings I have for myself.

I came to A.A. because I was tired of using myself and other people. I was sick and tired of feeling totally alone and useless. I thought no one liked me, and I certainly did not like myself. But the decisive impetus to join A.A. was an out-of-the-closet gay man who worked in my real estate office. I was simultaneously terrified and thrilled by his openly gay and confident nature, and by his apparent happiness and freedom as a gay man. I was also green with envy, and I wanted what he had. This man told me, once, that he was a member of A.A. He also said that he was a member of the local gay Nautilus health center. In March 1986, I did the easier, less threatening thing for me and joined the gym. A month later, when I was starting to look good on the outside, I was ready to tackle the hard part of feeling good on the inside. I was not sure there was any hope for me, but I felt compelled to try. The alternative was to kill myself. Though I was probably too scared to actually commit suicide, the fact that I seemed preoccupied with the idea indicates that I was at the bottom of depression. With a tremendous amount of fear, I picked up the telephone and called my friend. I remember the conversation as though it were yesterday. I simply said: "Help!" I felt totally defeated. Here I was...this upper class snob from Chicago's Gold Coast totally beaten. I had lost all my dignity and self-respect through drinking. But I recognized I could no longer control my life. My stubborn nature had to give way to some unknown solution.

My first day in A.A., I discovered that the solution was God. I did not have a problem accepting God as a solution to all my problems; I was delighted. What I had to get over, however, was the impression that my Higher Power was the vengeful deity I had been raised to believe in and to fear.

Today, God is my best friend. We camp it up together. Sometimes I feel that God is telling me: "Get over yourself, Mary! And I don't mean the Virgin! You're certainly not that, honey!" I seek daily help from my Creator and from His other children, who are now my best friends in A.A. These people are my family. I love them very much, and I am healed through their good, healthy examples. Through A.A. I've acquired self-esteem, and I can keep my ego properly proportioned, neither inflated nor deflated.

I accept my biological family, too, and I love them deeply. After much analysis and soul searching, I now can love my parents as they are. I accept the job they did raising me and loving me as the best that they could do. I have personally thanked my father and mother for having raised me. But I've also accepted the reality that I will never find the direction and love I always wanted from them; they simply did not and do not have it to offer. That kind of care and nurturing I receive in my A.A. family.

I am deeply grateful for all the good things and many blessings God has given me and, otherwise, allowed me to search out and find. My life is full and beautiful today. Absolutely all of my needs are met today through my

Higher Power. I simply have to remember to remain teachable and open to change, and to remember that acceptance is the answer to all my problems. I now can return the love and strength that my new and wonderful friends have given me through the program of A.A. I pray that everyone who enters the doors of this fellowship will reap the rewards with which I have been so abundantly blessed.

I know I can grow and continue to be healed only if I remember that the past is just that. What happened yesterday is gone for ever. It need never return, if I do not allow it to. My Higher Power has given me only today in which to work and to enjoy my life. I believe it is my goal and my duty to clear my mind of my will and to attempt to do God's will, remembering I can only do what He wills for me in His always appropriate timetable.

23

A Pauper No More

As always on Saturday night, I went out to get the newspaper. That walk saved my life. The store was only several hundred feet around the corner from our Greenwich Village apartment. My lover often was not at home. More and more I was alone, drunk, in the apartment. Alone because my lover of many years, more and more needed to get away from me, the drunk.

I went out to get the paper, but the next morning I woke up in St. Vincent's Hospital with my arms and legs in restraints, my right arm in a cast, and an oxygen mask over my face. But I was alive. While going for the paper, I had a sudden grand mal type seizure which alcoholics can sometimes get. When it hit, I fell over on the sidewalk, yelling and thrashing about. A passing police car scooped me up and dropped me off at the hospital.

I broke my arm thrashing about; thus the cast. Before the hospital could interrupt the seizure, I used up almost all of my energy. The almost fatal energy loss resulted in my contracting pneumonia, thus an oxygen mask.

If I had been alone in the apartment, the people downstairs would have heard banging and thumping and then, silence. If someone had not slipped protection under my head while I was thrashing about...If a police car had not been passing by...If the hospital had been miles, instead of blocks...If I had been smoking in bed...If...If...But I was alive. In the hospital, the physician was frank: "Don't drink." I understood.

I had been giving myself the usual line, "I don't drink too much." But every morning I came back from the liquor store with my liter of vodka, clutching it with both arms so as not to drop it with my shakes. Vodka for breakfast, vodka for lunch, vodka for supper; "Not too much," I told myself.

I did all the things drunk gay men do. Mornings I came to in unknown beds all over New York City and in neighboring states. Once, someone beating me up brought me to. One winter afternoon I came to floating down the Hudson River, wondering casually about my pea coat getting waterlogged and heavy. There I was floating down a winter river ready to sink at any moment, yet thinking that I was in control of the situation.

No. I was not drinking too much: Jail only once, but not my fault. Several times in the hospital, but only the emergency room. I lost only one job. My lover still loved me, though he stayed away a lot.

How did it come about that I was slowly committing suicide? Why was I so unprepared for life? Let me tell you about my grandmother, the "General" - a sweet old lady; a manipulating, emasculating guilt-giver. I understand her a little, now that she is dead many years.

In my family were my grandfather who died in '47, my mother who died in '57, and my grandmother who lived on and on. The family was bright, which meant problems were handled though the head, not through emotions. My grandmother ruled the family by pathological techniques: lying, pouting, self-pitying, and especially dishing out guilt. "Have you no respect for..." "After all that I have done for you..." "Your mother was such a good little girl, why can't you..." The General controlled our lives so much there was no spontaneity. Always places were set for supper at five o'clock, no changes considered, no exceptions allowed. While I was in the Army, I once got home on the city bus late, almost midnight. My grandmother was out on the sidewalk waiting for me. She said, "Everything has its place and everything in its place." Her attitude toward life was perfection for protection: "Suppose someone comes over." "What would the neighbors say." All the stories she told were of how wonderful she was. All my childhood achievements were only fodder for her self-serving stories. I hated it. She was obsessed with presenting a respectable public appearance. No emotions.

Certainly, never be angry - better to be depressed; silence is the more presentable disposition. No wonder that one carry-over to my present life is not to feel emotions - not to acknowledge or express them. I am trying now to learn not to bury anger. Another carry-over is chronic, low-level depression. One way to deal with that has been to run away, literally, as to Alaska. Alcohol was another excellent escape. Now a mechanism I use is to surround myself with barriers, as with the clutter of unfinished tasks. These barriers serve as loud music does for teenagers, barriers to emotions, especially anger.

In the family, my mother tried to be a filter, a shield between my grandmother and me. She was only fifty when she died. Her addiction to my grandmother killed her. I was in the army when Mother's physician told her that she had a tumor and needed an immediate operation. My grandmother said, "No. Let us pray." Mother followed the General's orders. Being the shield, Mother never wrote me about this. Mother eventually had the operation some months later, but the delay proved to be fatal. For the increasing pain, Mother was prescribed medicine. But my grandmother said, "No. Let me read to you from the Good Book." Mother followed the General's orders. Mother felt too guilty to take her pain medicine. My mother died, painfully. That is how powerful the General was. Before her own death, my grandmother picked out her own burial clothes and gave directions as to how to run her own funeral.

I learned about God - a Sunday necessity. I learned about drinking - wines at holidays. I learned about sex - the first time I was alone in bed exploring at the appropriate age. I did not know what was going on. Then, suddenly...What was all that sticky stuff? I thought maybe I was sick. Should I wake up my mother to tell her? But nothing hurt, so I decided to wait until morning.

I was a sex moron. In the Boy Scouts, a guy experimenting wanted to give me a blow job. It had happened to him, and he wanted to explore it with me. I really didn't know what a blow job was, but I thought it must be bad and dangerous; after all, girls got pregnant from sex, didn't they? As I said, I was unprepared for life.

When did I recognize I was gay? I don't know. In high school, I dated girls and had sex with boys, but did both only occasionally. And it remained only occasionally through college and during my time in Alaska. But when I moved to New York City, the anonymity meant promiscuous sex. At the bar you sized up what you wanted for the night. It was the ideal time to act like that; antibiotics for syphilis were on the scene, and AIDS was not. Liking women would not have kept me from liking vodka, but liking vodka did not make me like women.

The early evening of March 15th (now 14 or 15 years ago) I walked into Charlie's East and a man whom I'll call "Claude" was sitting on a bar stool. It was love at first sight for both of us. Although he's black and I'm white, and although he's 15 years younger than I, we've been together ever since.

Neither of us functioned with great emotional maturity. I had a series of marginal jobs. One of those jobs I kept for seven years until the vodka and I were fired. Claude liked studying at trade schools. He is very bright, but at regular work he's not so hot. Among our more serious problems were that I did not handle Claude's financial dependency very well. I also let him browbeat me. For example, I would make a second or third trip to the supermarket to get the specific size and brand of canned vegetables that he wanted for supper, and I screamed inside all the way.

After I was fired for drinking, I really started drinking. What spurred me on were no time obligations and my retirement nest egg.

As I drank, I became a great burden on Claude. When I was sprawled out drunk, he felt abandoned. Each time he returned to the apartment, he would be in terror of finding me battered and bloody. In fact, he did find me like that again and again; I fell down a lot. He pleaded with me not to wet the bed. When he couldn't take my growing incontinence, he moved to the couch. For me, now, that period in our relationship is like a nearly wordless chapter in a book; I remember so little because I was drunk so much of the time.

My drinking made Claude crawl the wall. But only the vodka counted for me. If he had cried or made scenes, if had he even brought in priests, rabbis, and chanting Buddhist monks, it would have meant only more guilt, prompting me to get more vodka. My world revolved around drinking. And drinking centered on me. Only when I was drinking did I feel in control.

Claude tried very hard to create pleasantness, to avoid scenes, to bring up positive prospects. He lectured me on self-love. Claude handled the situation, I think, as well as any human could have. But for his own sanity, he had to spend more and more time away. And more and more, I disappeared into the bottle.

While I was in the hospital following my seizure, the lease on our apartment expired. I had been wanting to return to my childhood home in Miami, but it is now as maddening a megalopolis as New York City. The closest thing to home was a nearby small town, a warm place where the men go naked to the waist.

I arrived here with almost no money and my arm in a cast. I stuck close to the A.A. clubhouse because there I had free coffee which I loaded with sugar - better than nothing. Luckily, the clubhouse soon offered me the custodian's job.

When I came to A.A., I was a spiritual pauper. I am no longer a pauper, but I am only now learning how spiritually rich I am. I've discovered that in A.A. here, it is very much easier to be gay than to be an atheist. If other people benefit by having "God", fine. I remind them to pray, to ask for guidance and to practice gratitude. I remind people of the A.A. slogans. I work the Twelve Steps by taking their essence and adopting them into my daily living. At the close of meetings, I hold hands. As others do their thing, I do my thing: I mentally strip the men. The closing slogan: "It works when you work it" - takes on new meaning.

I try to practice gratitude. I owe my life to A.A. I did not quit drinking because a voice boomed out of a lavender cloud saying, "You just stop that now. Hear?!" I quit because I was scared. Without A.A., even after my seizure, I would have slipped and slipped and slipped away. In A.A., people say you have to do what you have to do. If today is determined by yesterday, and tomorrow is determined by today, then I just stretched it out in both directions into some type of predestination. Hawking said something to the effect that at the big bang, God could have determined the laws of the universe and within those laws, that the universe has been running automatically ever since. Ellerbee says, "And so it goes." I think that I get syphilis not because God failed, or that I avoided a traffic ticket not because God smiled. Facing the world is scary. Routines and rituals are decision-free, guilt-free, and familiar. It would be a lot easier to believe that, if I obeyed the 12-point Scout Law, I would go to the happy hunting ground with 12 big boy scouts. Marx said that the idea of God is comforting. But comforting, too, is having a drink.

A while ago, it dawned on me that I was going to die. At first I fought the idea by searching for immortality. For me the search was difficult because I have no ongoing institutions to identify with, no church, no lodge, no school. Nor have I any children to carry on my memory if not necessarily my name. What I have is today. This small sliver of time is what it is all about, and that is all there is.

First, I sought immortality by imitating Rembrandt, by painting. Then I sought it by writing. At neither was I successful. But now I am beginning to accept my mortality. Humans are like clouds. Each cloud is different. Clouds form, cast their shadows, and rain, and then go away. They have been doing this for quite a while now. Humans, like clouds, will go on long after I die. Someday Claude will take my shoes down to the Salvation Army, and someone else will fill them. But for today, I can enjoy. One day at a time. It's a good principle to follow. Today, the clouds. Today, working the A.A. program. Today, sobriety. It's been "one day at a time" going on five years now. For the richness this has brought to my life, I know that I'm not a pauper.

24

The Actor

I remember when I was asked to tell my story for the first time. It wasn't until three days before my first A.A. birthday. I remember that as my first few months in A.A. passed with no one asking about my life before sobriety, my resentment began to build. I knew that my story was the most unique and interesting one ever heard. Well, I've told my story many times since then, and the thing I'm reminded of each time I tell it is how really ordinary it is. I'm just a regular garden variety drunk. But several new issues have come up in my life in the past year, so maybe my story is at least interesting now.

I was born into and raised by a middle class family in the 1940's. My parents owned a neighborhood grocery store, and we lived in a house which was connected to the rear of the store.

My earliest recollection of my parents is of them standing in the bedroom, yelling at each other at the top of their lungs and grabbing me out of each other's arms. Every time my father would snatch me, I would reach out for my mother. Growing up, I often thought that life for all of us would be better if my mother left my father, so that just mother and I could live together, and I could take care of her. Realistically, however, it would not have been a solution.

I was very much a loner as a child. On all my report cards from kindergarten, the teacher always remarked: "Does not get along well with others." I'm afraid, that's still largely true today, though I continue to work on this personal shortcoming.

In school, I was always called a sissy. I preferred playing jump rope or jacks with the girls, or re-enacting the latest Saturday morning serial, than playing ball with the guys. How disconcerting it was to think I might have to catch a ball. To this day, I'm still not fond of sports, except for ice hockey.

I didn't care for school too much and I was just an average student. The only time I studied was the night before an exam, when I'd memorize everything and then promptly forget it as soon as the exam was taken. I didn't see how math, history and geography were going to help me in the real world, because I was going to be the biggest movie star ever to hit the silver screen. I don't know how I thought I was going to become this major motion picture idol, being the very shy child that I was. Living in a fantasy world, as I did then and for much of my life, practical consideration usually seemed to elude one.

The day after I was graduated from high school, I went into the Navy. Nine months later, I told my superiors that I was a homosexual so that I could get out. I felt I was wasting my time in the Navy. I wanted to get on with being a star.

I went to New York, then to Hollywood. After neither of those showbiz meccas discovered me, I returned to my home in Texas and started studying drama at the local junior college. I lasted one semester, thought I was good enough for New York, and hit the road again. This was the beginning of a pattern of transiency that lasted for years.

There were a lot of job leads to follow and a fair number of actual jobs that took me all across the nation: tours of shows and some television and film work. All the time my drinking was escalating into the disease of alcoholism. I was always sitting on a barstool, talking about what I was going to accomplish and how I could do a better role than whoever happened to be doing it at the time, but never staying off the stool long enough to pursue my ambitions.

Of course, I doubt that I could have done any role better than whoever was playing it at the time. A really good actor needs feelings, passion and compassion. But I was slowly numbing everything an actor needs. I was dealing strictly on the most superficial of emotional levels. That neither stands one in good stead as an actor, nor as a human being.

I was always quick to blame directors, producers, casting agents and agents, or anyone else I could think of for my not getting hired. To look within myself to find the problem? Huh! It was always their fault. If only they would give me a job, I would be able to get my life together and everything would be all right. No, the jobs were not coming. My life kept getting more and more unbearable, lonelier, more miserable and more unmanageable.

Many times I "retired" from showbiz and started working as a bartender. It was the only job I wanted because I could support my habit by working in a bar. And when I couldn't get a job as a bartender, I'd take anything in a bar just so I could be near the booze and the glamor of the night life.

I was working as a waiter and a janitor in a bar and, one day on my day off, I went bar hopping, spending my just cashed pay check, buying drinks for everyone and trying to impress them, when I decided to pull a practical joke on the man who was sitting at the bar in front of me. I must have been in a partial blackout, because one minute I was thinking about how hilarious it would be if I poured a bowl of popcorn on this man's head, and the next minute I had already done it. I believe I was the only one who laughed.

The bartender was out from behind the bar in a shot, and, the next thing I knew, I was on the barroom floor looking up at him after he had knocked me down. I was promptly thrown out of the bar. At first I was bewildered; then, my cup overflowed with shame, remorse and embarrassment. I proceeded to drink the rest of that day all over town, until the bars closed at 2:00 a.m. By that time, I had blown my entire paycheck.

I spent the next five days in isolation, thinking about moving or killing myself. I had a history of thinking about suicide, but I think it was the sense of high drama of the act that appealed to me, more than the act itself. I don't think I actually could have taken my own life. Thinking about killing myself was really just an exercise in self-pity. In any case it happened that somehow, for the first time in my life, the realization hit me that I could no longer run away, because no matter where I went, I'd still be there. It was a disturbing but important insight.

Finally, I guess I just had had enough, and I went to talk with a lesbian minister friend of mine and asked her for help. Her first question to me was, "Do you think you have a problem with alcohol?" That was the beginning of the destruction of my wall of denial. I answered, "Yes."

The day I walked into my first meeting of Alcoholics Anonymous, I also moved into a halfway house run by my lesbian minister friend and her lover. They immediately dubbed me their honorary "dikette."

I did the usual moaning during my first year of sobriety, but I stayed sober. It was a long year, but I helped the time pass by getting involved in A.A. related activities during my first thirty days of sobriety. I volunteered to help out on the refreshment committee for a fund raising dance; I was the only person to volunteer. When the chairperson had to drop off the committee, I was the committee and in charge of all the refreshments. I was thrilled; no one had trusted me to do anything like this in a long time. I was even entrusted with the money, and I didn't steal it! On the day of the dance, I got a bunch of guys together, who had come into the program about the same time as I had, and we got into the kitchen and diced, chopped, sliced and played Connie Casserole with gay abandon. What can I say...it kept us sober. I also made coffee, cleaned ashtrays, chaired meetings - anything I had to do to stay sober.

The biggest thrill of that year was when I celebrated my first year birthday in Montreal at the 50th International Conference. That was a natural high I don't think I'll ever forget. And I was able to share that experience with my mother, who is in Al-Anon in order to support me in my recovery.

I'll soon be celebrating another A.A. milestone. This past year has been the roughest of my sobriety. I lost my sister to a heart attack. I lost several friends to AIDS. I discovered that I had been living in denial regarding my father's own alcoholism. I discovered that I'm co-dependent (though I'd always thought I was too independent to be a candidate for this category). I've been trying to get back into show business on a professional level, but without much success - YET. I've been under treatment for depression which, considering what's been happening to me, should be no surprise. But it came as a surprise to me. I was depressed for six months before I even knew it - someone had to tell me. I've contracted bursitis in my shoulder (my doctor tried to tell me as tenderly as possible that people at my age start to get physical disorders of this type, but I knew what he meant). I've had friends abandon me because they couldn't handle my depression and my talks of drinking and suicide. I tried religion, again, and lost my faith - again. I cursed God and get mad at God a lot. Things seemed so bad that I even spent a day in the lock-up ward in a hospital, but the staff didn't think I was crazy enough to keep. I didn't think so either, after that experience. I didn't know if I felt more like Jack Nicholson in "One Flew Over The Cuckoo's Nest" or Natalie Wood in "Splendor in the Grass" - probably more like Natalie Wood....at least she got better.

But through all of this, I have stayed sober. I still ask God in the morning to keep me sober and thank Him at night when He does, even if most of the time I believe that God, or the Higher Power - or whatever - is a crock. I've gone through most of the past year feeling helpless and hopeless, just as I did in my first year of sobriety .

But I'm starting to get back some faith-blind faith, as it were. I have some hope that, since the things I used to do worked once, maybe they'll work again. I have no idea what all lies ahead for me, but I do know that by staying sober I at least will have a chance of choosing the steps I take and of accomplishing some of what I would like to accomplish as I trudge down the road of happy destiny.

25

Long Distance Sobriety

There was a time in my life that I thought I, Cliff, was the only person alive. Feeling so alone and afraid, I turned to what I thought was my best friend, alcohol. It didn't matter what size bottle or what brand; as long as whatever it was had alcohol in it, I loved it.

When I drank I was no longer lonely. I thought drinking made me feel good. I drank daily for many years, unaware of where time was going. I only knew I had to drink to feel good. Through all the pain and misery of my drinking, I managed to make an attempt at living a normal life.

In February 1985, I was starting to hit my bottom with alcohol. I was alone on my birthday, February 17, and feeling especially lonely when an ad in a magazine I was reading caught my eye. It read something to the effect that if you are lonely and want to talk to someone, you should call this number. So I called. I was connected to a party line based in California. People were calling from all over the country. I heard a man's voice and started talking to him. I asked this person for his name; it was Mark. Mark sounded like a nice guy, so we exchanged numbers, and I called him back at home. Mark lived in San Francisco. There was something special about his voice. He was across the country, but he sounded so close. Mark didn't know it at the time, but he was going to be my new friend. He was put into my life for a reason that, at the time, neither of us was aware of.

I started to call Mark on a daily basis for the next six months. After a few months, Mark shared with me that he was sober in A.A. for five years. I really had no idea what he meant. Most of the time, when I spoke with Mark, I was drinking. This A.A. business didn't interest me at all, so I continued to drink for another few months.

In late October, I no longer had a friend in alcohol. It turned against me. The only friend I knew I had was a guy named Mark who was across the country. By this time Mark and I had grown close. I called Mark, as I usually did, when I was in pain and needed someone to talk to. I asked Mark if he could help me. I told him I couldn't continue to drink the way I was. I knew that if I were to continue, I would die. Mark asked me if I was ready to stop drinking, and I answered that I was. He talked with me and calmed me down. He told me about A.A. here in New York City. The next day, I called the A.A. intergroup and asked for the locations and times of A.A. meetings. I went to my first meeting and have been sober since.

This past June (1987) I decided that it was time to meet Mark. I made plans to attend the gay A.A. round up, "Living Sober," in San Francisco and to meet Mark while there. Going to San Francisco was a beautiful experience. I not only got to meet Mark, I met myself. While attending "Living Sober," I was with 4000 other gay people recovering in A.A. This in itself was a spiritual experience. I was with people whom I understood and who understood me.

"Living Sober" was a powerful example of how God speaks through people. In California I accepted three things in my life: the first was people, the second was the A.A. program, and the third was a higher power whom I chose to call God.

Since returning to New York, I have been a different person. I left the old Cliff behind and brought the new Cliff home. I had found serenity and started to live a joyful, sober life.

I am very grateful to A.A. for my sobriety, and to "Living Sober-'87" for showing me the way. But I am especially grateful to an alcoholic in San Francisco whose name is Mark and whose patience, understanding and good will brought me to a new life.

26

Short Story

For me, it all began when I was in elementary school. I was the kid that was picked last for the team, the one who walked around the school yard with his only two friends there. God forbid if those two were ever sick on the same day. I remember looking at those kids that were popular. What made them popular? Why were they and not I? One common link seemed to run through them all...drugs.

When I reached the 9th grade I entered into high school. I made a promise to myself to never be that dork of a kid that hung out under the principal's window during recess. I was going to be popular and accepted at any cost. So I got heavy into drugs! I was instantly accepted, I was "cool."

My high school years were fairly normal in the area of girls. I dated often and had several girlfriends. I enjoyed sex and had that often with my girlfriends. Still, I was always aware of my interest in boys. As far back as age five, I remember my attraction to them in a physical way. I always thought that it was just a passing phase.

About seven months into sobriety, I met a friend in A.A. who was gay. He talked about what it was like to be gay and I listened with fascination. I had never met an openly gay person before. I realized that I related a lot with what he was saying. Later that week, I spent two weeks at his home while his parents were out of town, and that was my grand coming out celebration.

My friend held a Halloween party and invited several gay people over. I loved it from the start. I felt I had finally found my place. Gay life turned out to be fun, friendly and meaningful.

About nine months into sobriety, I became involved

in a serious relationship with another man in the program. He was everything I thought I wanted at the time. Things progressed quickly and soon we were living together. Talk about insanity - two newly sober, newly out gay alcoholics were living together. Needless to say, it was interesting. Luckily, I had found gay A.A. This group was to help me out in so many ways. I found the support and openness I had never found before. I was finally able to speak openly without fear of rejection solely based on my sexual orientation. I found a sponsor in the gay A.A. group. I found holiday activities and other sober events to participate in and this made my sobriety much easier for me.

After about three years of being in this relationship with my lover, we broke up. It was difficult at first, being in the same area and going to the same meetings, but I think the program helped us work through that.

Today, my ex-lover and I are very good and close friends. We are a great support to each other and even provide companionship when we need a dinner date or a movie date. I can't see having such a relationship with him now without the program in both our lives. I owe much to A.A. and the group - without gay A.A., I don't think I would be as well as I am today.

27

Gifts

In January 1943, I was born in the panhandle of Oklahoma, under the sign of Capricorn. My father was very much excited about my birth, as he had six daughters, and he very much wanted a son. In the traditional manner in which a father celebrates the birth of his child, mine was celebrated by passing out cigars. A man stopped him and told him that he should not be so proud. When asked why not, the man replied, "You had to take two to get him." The truth is that I was the first born of triplets, with the other two being girls. When I was born, I already had four older sisters who were each born two years apart and a set of twin sisters who were two years older than I. My youngest sister was born two years after I was. I was raised with nine sisters, a mother, a grandmother, which is a total of eleven women.

I am a third generation alcoholic on my paternal side. I have two generations of alcoholism on my maternal side. I've been active in Al Anon from the time I just started A.A. in March 1977. I am also active in N.A. (Narcotics Anonymous), S.A. (Sexaholics Anonymous), and A.C.O.A. (Adult Children of Alcoholics). I am basically an obsessive-compulsive person, but today I have an accepting attitude and continue to work on myself.

What's it like to be the only male child raised in a family of eleven women you ask.... well, you play softball as soon as you can walk. We had a girl's softball team, and I was the coach, the waterboy and the cheerleader. (I preferred being the cheerleader). We never had to go across the street to get any players. I was the only boy in third grade who knew that a D & C was not just an electrical current and I was a freshman in college before I had any Bayer aspirin. With nine sisters, your mother buys Midol by the case. A distinct advantage of my situation in the family was that I never had to wear hand-me-downs.

When I was four I had my first experience drinking alcohol. I had located my grandmother's cough medicine and had talked my triplet sisters into sampling the entire bottle with me. That led to turning cartwheels and throwing up in the front yard. Our neighbor lady called our mother and told her we were sick. Forty years later, I have a solution to that sickness.

At a very early age, I was treated special by my father. He took me hunting, fishing, and to work with him. He spent a lot of quality time with me. I was treated special by everyone around me. I had one of those super Christmases when, at the age of three, I was gotten up at 3:00 a.m. to play with my new twenty-two foot electric train set with just my father and my mother. Each evening I was put to bed with my father and, then, when I went to sleep, my mother would put me in my own bed. (This, I believe, led to male bonding patterns later in my life).

I learned at an early age, that I was special, and that made me want others to love me, to need me, and to know I was special. So I learned to be an achiever to retain my specialness. In high school I was in fourteen organizations at once and an officer in all of them. I was the Chapter Star farmer in Oklahoma, and I did not even live on a farm. I was high point man in state track for four years in a row. Performance-based society had nothing on me that I could not accomplish.

My father died when I was five, leaving my mother with the financial responsibility of raising ten children and caring for a live-in grandmother. My mother was a bookkeeper and my father had worked for Oklahoma Gas and Electric. We also owned a bar, and this provided a very sufficient income for our family. When my father died of cirrhosis of the liver, things changed. Mother kept the bar until I was in the third grade, whereupon she became a county court clerk. Our income went from $3000.00 per month to $365.00 per month, so everyone went to work at an early age. Before Dad died we were raised with three cars, baby-sitters, a maid and a gardener; then, all this changed.

Mother treated each person like a piece of office equipment. None of us children were treated by her with real feelings of being loved. I think, maternally speaking, she had never learned a concept of love from her own family, because my grandmother was very much like her. I never knew my mother's father, so I can't speak about him. My mother's parents had eight children, and often I speculate that it simply means that they had sex only eight times. We children were close to each other, but always yearning for some special individual maternal attention, which was never forthcoming. It was in this kind of familial environment that I recognized I was homosexual -- that my sexual feelings and fantasies were different from what they were supposed to be for a male. I kept this knowledge a secret from everyone. Even after my close friends knew that I was gay, I was the last person to accept that fact.

My military and college experiences found me again performance bound and energetic in achieving. In college, my undergraduate degree was in Housing and Interior design. At first, I was quite straight-laced. I remember one Friday evening I went to a bar with a bunch of guys from the dorm. There were two policemen in the bar, and I did not drink anything, remembering that I could not do anything in public to embarrass myself or others. I was informed from an early age that men held their liquor. They did not pass out, spend the night in jail, or throw up in public, so I practised not doing those things.....which isn't to say that alcohol and I didn't become rather quickly acquainted. Actually, alcohol and I had a wonderful marriage in college. I seemed to be better looking and my abilities to dance and communicate were easier. Scoring was wonderful. Alcohol did for me what no other thing ever did. It was fantastic, but this would change. It was while I was at college that I also came out.

I should note that I was raised as a Southern Baptist. Baptists do not smoke, drink, or dance in public, so, to remove the guilt, I became a member of the Episcopal church. They do smoke, drink and dance in public. But after I came out, I found myself doing things that Episcopalians do not do, so I just quit going to church altogether. I prayed to God especially in times of high stress or crisis, but answers were not heeded or paid attention to at this time.

When I graduated from Oklahoma "Straight" University, my first move was to San Francisco. While there, I got into S & M relationships (and this was not Standing and Modeling!) In my fear I moved away and ended up in Houston, Texas, where I had my first intimate relationship. What was a trick stayed for nine years. We learned to drink, party and play together.

We later moved to Southern Oklahoma. I went into business for myself, and we lived in the country. I raised Arabian and half-Arabian show horses as a hobby, which was paid for by my lucrative design business. My financial goal was to be a millionaire by the time I was thirty, which, in fact, I became, but in a queer way. Five years after the move to Oklahoma, my drinking forced me to go out of business. My property sold for more than a million dollars at a sheriff's auction. As my business boomed, so did my drinking — to one-half gallon of Weller's bourbon a day. I had to use Librium to keep my hands from shaking. I was losing control, but I could not accept that fact.

In July, 1975 a friend of mine phoned and wanted to visit. I was doing the design work on his house at the time and having a lot of problems with his wife. He came to see me and wanted me to tell him of my problems, but I could not be honest with him. After he left, my lover asked what he had wanted, and I said that he wanted me to tell him that I was an alcoholic, but that I could not say this. I would not allow myself to say the word or acknowledge the fact in any way.

In September, 1976, I woke up in a Dallas hospital from an acute pancreatic attack that had begun four days before. The physician told me that I could not drink for three months. (He also said that I should never drink again. He was right, but some of us learn more slowly than others.)

December found my relationship on the rocks and separation in order. I had been barred from all the bars in Dallas for a year due to my physical violence, and I didn't even live in Dallas. After one particularly nasty fight with my lover, I ended up planning on going to San Francisco for a two week cure of booze and orgies. I left work, telling my boss (I was no longer self-employed) that it was either that or a nervous breakdown. The truth was that I was about to be fired. It is typical that alcoholics don't think they are fired because of their drinking behavior.

I didn't go to San Francisco, but bought a quart of Weller's, and went to see my dog. I had a ninety-seven pound Alpha Doberman Pinscher that my mother was taking care of for me. On my way to see my dog, I picked up a hitchhiker who'd been released from prison only twenty-four hours before. We partied to Oklahoma City where I took him to my sister's. She promptly called everyone in my family over, and they persuaded me to take him to a motel for the night. I spent the evening with him, having $6000.00 on my person, and left him there in the morning with only $10.00 in my pocket. I went on to the panhandle to see my dog.

For some reason, I cried a lot while at my mother's, and I didn't drink for the two weeks I was there. I knew something was really wrong. I went back to Oklahoma City, and my oldest sister (who had divorced her husband thirteen years earlier for alcoholism) told me the friend that had come to visit me the summer before was in Alcoholics Anonymous and had been in A.A for the past four and a half years. She told me that I was going to go have a cup of coffee with him and talk. I was thirty-three and had never had a cup of coffee in the evening in my life.

It was a very frightening experience. I didn't know what to do or what to say. He asked me in, offered me coffee, and gave me the "Big Book." He told me that he wanted me to do myself a favor and to go to an A.A. meeting the first chance I had. He told me that I would have to change my playgrounds and playmates, that I was an intelligent person and that I was going to find out about a simple program to keep me sober. He then hugged me and wished me luck. I thought he was crazy.

I moved back to Houston. Through the grapevine, I found out that Lynn, a woman I had partied coast to coast with, was sober in A.A. for the past year and a half. She was in town, and we became reacquainted. She introduced me to marijuana. I was in love again. My vision was affected, but my cock got hard, and again life seemed easy. But this was not to last long. Paranoid behavior set in within three months, so drug substitution did not work.

On March 14, 1977, my friend, Lynn, took me to a couple's home for dinner and to my first A.A. meeting. The couple, Ralph and Shary, were happy, laughing people and in A.A. I was convinced that they were on speed, as well as everyone at the A.A. meeting. It was not an accident that the topic of the session was fear. A frizzy-haired lesbian (this was a regular meeting at the then Travis Club in Houston) was fearful of a man getting in her apartment. I had a fear that a man would *not* get in my apartment, much less rape me. I prayed. After the meeting Ralph asked me what I was afraid of. I simply told him, "Of snakes." That was all.

On Monday, March 17, 1977, Ralph took me to my first meeting at Lambda, which had three meetings a week in the Unitarian church in Houston. Again, the meeting was on fear. Eight of the eleven men there were professional designers, and one of them hurt my feelings by telling me that he had been saving a chair for me for years. I recovered quickly and said that they should have saved me a chaise lounge, I needed to lie down a lot.

This was the beginning of an incredible relationship with life, with myself and God, and with A.A. I would love to say that these relationships were and are without pain, but this is not true.

What got me on the road to recovery (and what still keeps me) was the second most important word in Alcoholics Anonymous, the word WE. It has the wonder of two of us doing together what the one of me cannot. It is the love of inclusion, of being included, as in the sponsor-sponsoree interaction in which the cleansing and healing process of being loved by the sponsor supports the sponsoree until he can begin to love himself.

In A.A. all personal action and change proceeds in a succession of steps. I believe in the first three steps that we wake up. In the next six steps, we grow up. And in the last three steps, we learn to stay up with our spiritual and human experience.

"Powerless" is an absolute word. It has no conditions, no alternatives. The first two steps of the program are admission and acceptance of being alcoholic --- of being powerless over alcohol. In accepting my own powerlessness over alcohol, I began to develop a constructive power. My life became manageable. The electric company does not disconnect your electricity when you pay the bill; this is management. Management is sometimes just getting out of bed. Learning to sleep without chemical use is management. Making coffee, even emptying ashtrays is management.

I came to believe that the power that created the entire universe created you and me. This creative power gave each one of us the power to make decisions and to know that everything is a choice. We learn to live with the consequences of those choices. This is the constructive power to which I was restored. A.A. has allowed me to be restored to happy, joyous and sane living. Through the A.A. program, I believe we are restored to whole health in our working, in our playing, and in our loving. I still have to work on my loving and playing lives.

I was in A.A. for two years when I went with friends to a Third Step meeting in Angeleton, Texas. About 100 members were present. An older man, who I thought was sleeping in the back of the room, suddenly announced that he believed that we were spiritual beings and that what we were learning was to have a HUMAN experience, one day at a time. This made sense to me. I accept the idea that we are all unique children of God. Alcoholics Anonymous is designed to handle the wounded child in each one of us. The Third Step allowed me to accept God as my primary caretaker, though I make a daily conscious decision to believe that.

My rejection of my Baptist and Episcopalian backgrounds made it difficult for me, at first, to believe in God. All I felt was contempt. But A.A. gave me permission to define God as I understood Him. This had never been granted to me before. Through A.A., I came to experience what for me is the reality -- that God is deep down in every man, woman and child.

The Fourth Step allowed me to realize that humans are made up of assets and liabilities. The growth I experienced in the Fourth Step enabled me to view my liabilities as potential assets, as opportunities for further personal growth.

The gifts I received in the Fifth Step were understanding, humility and compassion. Peace came to me, too, in the actual experience of talking with myself, with God, and with another human being about my weaknesses and failings, as well as about my strengths. The Fifth Step also gave definition to my short and long term goals.

GRACE is the gift realized from the Sixth and Seventh Steps. Grace is God's riches at Christ's expense. Sometimes God must bring us face to face with our weaknesses so that we can allow His will for us to be done. God's will is that I take my will and place it in agreement with God's intentions for me. These steps also brought me calm and peace.

In the Eighth Step I made a list of all the people I had wronged or hurt through my drinking. In the Ninth Step I made up to all these people (or tried to make up to these people as well as I could, or as well as they'd let me) for what I'd done to them when I'd been drinking. Each person does this in his own manner. There are no prescribed ways of making amends. The actual beauty of this step was that I learned not to give any power to my past. It was the beginning of accepting the fact that time is the healing factor in my life.

Enhanced human functioning was the benefit I real-

ized (and realize) from the daily inventory of my actions that is the Tenth Step. This is a wonderful experience in self-discipline. I find that the daily interrogation helps me maintain my integrity.

The value of the Eleventh Step for me was that I found a way to bring my mind in harmony with God's. The beauty of this step for me was that through prayer and meditation I had an avenue to self-discovery. I found that God's first gift was of me to myself. The second gift was of others, united by our drinking, by our desire to remain sober, and by our need and our care for each other. God's third gift was of faith and trust in Him and of hope that sobriety was there for me, if I chose it.

A.A. itself is a gift. The Twelfth Step comes from this awareness. As recovering alcoholics in A.A., we have received a life-saving and a life-renewing gift. With the realization comes the responsibility to share, even to be, this gift for others. This is what the Twelfth Step means to me.

Alcoholics Anonymous teaches us in our own manner of learning and relearning to live our lives with Style, Dignity and Grace. Style is the manner in which we present ourselves each day (with our practice of the Twelve Steps of A.A.). Our Dignity is our ability to be responsible in our working, in our playing and in our loving. Grace is the beautiful experience of God as we each understand God to be, and of His blessings for us as His children.

My story tells you that I am a very ordinary man, but that with one drink of alcohol, one joint, or one line of coke, I become a beast. Today it is my choice to be an ordinary man. I know today that I am worthy of self-love and self-acceptance. I enjoy being me, and growing is an exciting part of my daily experience. I accept that I have power over only this moment and have learned not to run away as often from life or to fight life as hard as I did before I chose A.A. and sobriety.

In October 1986, I was terminated from my state job as a psychologist. I, in turn, sued the state and won back my rights to be a productive individual. The week I was fired, I came down with a positive AIDS Related Complex diagnosis, having eleven of the fifteen symptoms. My experience with A.A. allowed me to minimize my fear over this. I accept that I am 100% responsible for everything I do to myself. In the program of Alcoholics Anonymous, I was able to learn to take proper care of myself. Two months ago, I was rediagnosed as only positive for the H.I.V. antibodies and was taken off medication. My doctor was happy, wanting to know how I was capable of this change. I do not have to tell you this answer. I just used A.A. and changed everything about myself. I am on a raw foods diet. I use visualization one and a half hours per day. My day has become a living meditation of listening to myself, to God, and of attending to the insights I've attained through A.A.

In closing, I would like to refer to this statement from the Big Book:

("The last fifteen years of my life have been rich and meaningful. I have had my share of problems, heartaches and disappointments, because that is life, but also I have known a great deal of joy, and a peace that is the handmaiden of an inner freedom. I have a wealth of friends and, with my A.A. friends, an unusual quality of fellowship. For, to these people, I am truly related. First, through mutual pain and despair, and later through mutual objectives and new-found faith and hope. And, as the years go by, working together, sharing our experiences with one another, and also sharing a mutual trust, understanding and love -- without strings, without obligation -- we acquire relationships that are unique and priceless.

There is no more "aloneness" with that awful ache, so deep in the heart of every alcoholic that nothing, before, could ever reach it. That ache is gone and need never return again.

Now there is a sense of belonging, of being wanted and needed and loved. In return for a bottle and a hangover, we have been given the Keys of the Kingdom.")

Alcoholics Anonymous – 3rd edition, 1976, p.312

[**Editor's Note:** This author died of AIDS in 1988]

For additional copies of this book or other publications of
WinterStar Press, write:

WinterStar Press
P.O. Box 199
North Liberty, Iowa 52317
USA

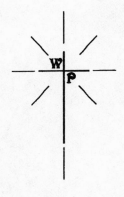

For additional copies of this book or other publication of interest please write:

Winterstar Press
P.O. Box 199
North Liberty, Iowa 52317
USA